how2become

How to Master the Teacher Interview Questions and Answers: 50 Questions and Answers

www.How2Become.com

D1342602

4 1 0260661 5

As part of this product you have also received FREE access to online tests that will help you to pass the tests to become a teacher.

To gain access, simply go to:

www.PsychometricTestsOnline. co.uk

Get more products for passing any test at:

www.How2Become.com

Orders: Please contact How2Become Ltd, Suite 14, 50 Churchill Square Business Centre, Kings Hill, Kent ME19 4YU.

You can order through Amazon.co.uk under ISBN: 9781910602959, via the website www.How2Become.com or through Gardners.com.

ISBN: 9781910602959

First published in 2016 by How2Become Ltd.

Typeset by How2Become Ltd.

Disclaimer

Every effort has been made to ensure that the information contained within this guide is accurate at the time of publication. How2Become Ltd is not responsible for anyone failing any part of any selection process as a result of the information contained within this guide. How2Become Ltd and their authors cannot accept any responsibility for any errors or omissions within this guide, however caused. No responsibility for loss or damage occasioned by any person acting, or refraining from action, as a result of the material in this publication can be accepted by How2Become Ltd.

The information within this guide does not represent the views of any third party service or organisation.

Contents page

Introduction

The teaching profession is now more varied than ever before. Modern teachers are more than just curriculum educators. They are role models, leaders and innovators; the first line of contact that our children have with a brighter and better future. With this in mind, it's essential that schools are employing the right type of people for the job.

In this book, we'll show you how to demonstrate that you ARE the perfect person for the role. We'll cover a wide variety of interview tips and techniques, show you the questions that you are most likely to be asked AND provide sample responses to show you the best ways to answer them.

By the end of this guide, you will be in a perfect position to ace your teaching interview, and secure your dream role.

The structure of this guide

To make things easier for you, this guide is broken down into useful sections. This reflects the way in which you should go about preparing for your interview. Taking a structured, organised, and thorough approach to your preparation will go a long way to helping you secure a position.

There are generally three parts to an interview, and we have covered all of these in extensive detail within this guide:

1. The 'getting to know you' section.

2. The competency-based question section.

3. The teaching section.

For each section, we'll provide you with a multitude of potential questions and full, in-depth example responses, to help you structure your answers in a way that impresses the interviewers. Before we get into the questions, we'll also run through the teaching core competencies, show you how to study a job description, and provide top tips to improve your chances of success.

In our first chapter, we'll look at the role of a teacher, give you some top interview preparation tips, and underline the importance of teacher core competencies – including what they are and how to apply them to your answers.

Chapter 1
Teacher Interview Preparation

Before you attend your teaching interview, it's imperative that you have a sustained knowledge of the following topics:

- What a teacher does, their role in school, and their responsibility towards students.

- What a teacher at the school YOU are applying to does, their role in school, and their responsibility towards students.

- Your subject, and why it matters in a wider context.

- The core competencies/expectations of a teacher.

- The policies of the school that you are applying to.

You'll be asked questions on all of these topics during the interview, so make sure you conduct a period of extensive research beforehand.

<u>There are two invaluable resources for you here:</u>

Firstly, you can use the website of the school to find a list of the school policies, expectations and guidelines. School websites usually have downloadable newsletters and lists of any key accomplishments/ awards they have received. Make sure you can bring knowledge of their history to the interview, because this will give you a crucial edge over other candidates.

Secondly, there is the job description itself. In the job description, you'll be given a list of requirements for the role. Make sure you pay close attention to these. A typical list might look like this:

SAMPLE

<u>The successful candidate will be able to:</u>

- Lead and communicate with students on a daily basis.

- Share knowledge and information with pupils of all age ranges.

- Take a leading role in promoting diversity and acceptance within the school environment.

- Act as a responsible adult and support figure for pupils and students who attend Ficshire High.

There are two ways of looking at this list. A weak candidate might look at the list and think 'check, check, check… I can do all of these things, I'll apply now.' They might not bother to read the list properly, and won't study it in preparation for the interview. A strong candidate, on the other hand, will look at the list differently. They'll break the skills required down into **behavioural competencies**.

For example:

Lead and communicate with students on a daily basis.

- This is clearly indicative of the fact that you will need great leadership skills, and must be a good communicator.

- Communication can be broken down into listening and responding to students.

- Leadership can also be broken down into taking initiative, making difficult decisions and acting responsibly.

As you might already be able to see, there is far more to a teacher's job description than what initially meets the eye, and each requirement can be broken down into smaller requirements. These requirements are known as core competencies, and will ALWAYS be assessed during the teacher interview.

The Core Competencies of Teaching

If you have been for any job interview in the past, you might be familiar with the term 'core competencies'. The core competencies refer to a set of behavioural standards required in the role of a teacher. Not only are there pre-existing requirements for teachers in general, but each school will also have particular competencies of their own – which they'll expect teachers to abide by.

In this section, we'll look at the general core competencies expected of teachers, and why they will be essential in your interview.

Listening

Listening is incredibly important for teachers. Unfortunately, when you are placed in charge of a class of 30 students, it can be extremely difficult. There are so many voices in the classroom that many new teachers become overwhelmed by the listening aspect of the role. This applies when you are one-to-one with a student too. In order to teach, you must be able to understand what knowledge needs to be imparted, and in order to do this you must be able to listen. Whether you are teaching children or adults, it's essential that your pupils are asking questions about the subject, and learning from your responses.

Relationship Management

The second core quality on our list is relationship management. Relationship management is all about resolving conflict and disagreement, and encouraging a good relationship between the teacher and pupil.

Remember that, particularly when dealing with teenagers and adolescents, conflict is an inevitable element of the classroom environment. Not everyone can get along all of the time. As a teacher, it is your job to prevent this from escalating. You must be able to provide a calm and reasonable support base, and must be someone who can look objectively at issues – in order to manage and resolve difficult peer-to-peer relationships.

Instructing

It goes without saying that instructing is an essential element of teaching. In order to become a teacher, you must be able to teach! This means you must be able to give clear instructions, impart your wisdom in a way that your pupils understand, and lead by example. It is no good having knowledge or behavioural skills, if you have no idea of how to apply them in the teaching environment.

The quality of your lessons will depend on your ability to deliver knowledge and information in a clear and concise fashion. The way this knowledge is delivered also needs to be engaging and interactive. You could have the clearest delivery possible, but if your students are unable to engage with your teaching methods, then they will find it extremely difficult to focus or learn.

Organisation

One of the most fundamental skills for any teacher to have is good organisation. Organisation will separate the good teachers from the bad, and many people would argue that this is actually the most important competency. Without good organisation and time management, you will really struggle to succeed as a teacher.

The most common complaint from teachers is that they just don't have enough time to complete all of the tasks that they need to. Teaching is the ultimate time consumer. The classroom environment is extremely difficult to manage, students don't always pay attention and it's easy to get side-tracked by a discussion/overrunning subject, or misbehaviour in the classroom. Furthermore, you'll have enormous amounts of marking to do, as well as lesson planning. The latter will severely eat into your free time, and ensure that you are maxed out in your career.

With all this, you should be able to see that organisation is absolutely essential. You need to take a systematic approach to your work, be disciplined in your methods, and understand what needs to be done and in what timeframe. It is inevitable that at some point in your career that you are going to feel overworked. Therefore, it's important that you minimise this as much as possible, in order to get the best out of yourself and your pupils.

Lesson Planning

You will become extremely familiar with lesson planning as you progress in your career. Lesson planning is absolutely vital. It will help you to stay organised, keep your classes on track, stay up-to-date with which classes still need to learn which material, and plan out every single day that you are teaching. The problem with this is that lessons don't always go to plan. In fact, it's extremely rare for a lesson to go exactly the way a teacher wants it to. Classroom disruptions, overrunning discussions, and slow students are all issues that will take away from the chances of your lessons running smoothly.

However, one of the great things about being a teacher is that no two days are the same. You will face a variety of different challenges, demands and questions on a daily basis. Once you start planning lessons, you'll really start to understand why your teachers used to get so frustrated with pupils who were disruptive. Every minute that you have to waste asking the class to settle down or behave, is a minute that you could have spent teaching.

The other reason that lesson planning is important is that it prevents you from running out of activities halfway through the lesson. No teacher wants to be caught with nothing to teach, but if the class whizzes through the material faster than expected, or simply isn't engaging, then sometimes this can happen. Games such as Hangman are a really useful way of filling in extra time, and are a great method of imparting useful knowledge and interacting with students.

Leadership

As the teacher, you are the leader of the class. Students will look up to you and require guidance. You will also act as the authority figure for the group, so you will need to be able to live up to this role.

It's true that some teachers, when they start out, might struggle with this. Leadership isn't for everyone, and it's often difficult to deal with at first. You might see yourself as a great teacher, but not necessarily a great leader.

However, the reality is that the two go hand-in-hand. Think about it like this; you want your students to learn from you and take on board the lessons you are teaching them. What is the best way to achieve this? The answer is to win their respect. If your students respect you, you'll have a far easier time teaching them.

Leadership involves almost all of the competencies on this list, and is a fundamental quality for teachers to have!

Professionalism

When you are employed as a teacher, it is essential that you can act with professionalism at all times. Teachers are there to set an example for their pupils, and therefore students must be able to look up to you. This means that your behaviour both inside and outside of the classroom needs to be exemplary. You must be able to act with integrity, and show a good level of respect to everyone.

As a teacher, an important part of your role is in practicing fairness and equality. Schools are culturally diverse places, and this means that everyone attending the school (staff or students) must be respectful of the differences between themselves and others, and treat every person that they meet in the same way. As a teacher, it's your job to enforce this, and show students the correct way to behave.

Why are these competencies important?

So, why are these competencies important? Well, apart from showing you how you need to behave as a teacher, they will also be fundamental during the interview.

As we've explained, the teaching interview is made up of 3 stages. The 2nd stage of the interview will not only test your knowledge of the competencies, but will also require you to demonstrate occasions where you have used these competencies in the past. For example, you might be asked to talk about a time when you have demonstrated your organisational skills.

In the interview section of this guide, we'll break down exactly how to do this.

Chapter 2
Teacher Interview
(Part 1)

The first part of your teacher interview will generally consist of 'getting to know you' type questions. What do we mean by this? Well, you'll be asked questions based on:

- Your research into the position.

- Your personality.

- Your subject knowledge and understanding of what makes a good teacher.

Since you'll be working with children, it's essential that the interviewers can get to know you properly, before they make a decision on whether to hire you. The school need to be assured that you are a safe and responsible individual, who can provide great leadership to their students. Although you will need to pass a DBS check anyway to gain a position as a teacher, it's important for the school to make certain beforehand. They don't just need to know that you are safe and trustworthy, but that you are reliable, hardworking, organised and able to cope under pressure.

Remember that when you are being interviewed for a teaching position, you aren't just being interviewed for any job. Teachers aren't just teachers; they are carers and role models, and therefore it's essential that schools choose the right candidate for the job. The last thing that a school wants is to employ someone who will crumble under pressure when faced with a class full of students. With this in mind, they need to make sure that they have a personality that fits with the role.

Throughout this chapter, we'll be showing you how to put this across in your answers. Our sample responses are aimed at helping teachers across any level. Whether you are a trainee applying for that first job or an experienced teacher, our answers are sure to help you.

Let's get started, by looking at some typical 'personality' type questions.

> **Q1. Tell us a bit about your skills, background and motivation for applying for this role.**

This gives you a chance to tell the interviewer about who you are as a person, what has led to your interest in teaching, and give some opening details about your skills and experience. It's a common way for most interviews to start. Essentially, you need to sell yourself to the interviewer. This question can make a huge difference to the way in which the rest of the interview goes; you will want to set a professional and enthusiastic tone. Of course, first impressions mean a lot, so make yours count.

Another important point to remember when it comes to answering this question is that you don't need to just talk about yourself. You can expect to be asked questions on your knowledge of the school, but try to briefly link your personal qualities with those of the school. For example, telling the school that you are someone who has worked with a number of charities, and that you know they are keen supporters of various charities and trusts, will link your ethos to theirs.

Schools want to hire someone who shares their values and believes in similar causes. Even at this early stage, showing that you have this quality will go a long way to securing the job position, and create a fantastic first impression.

Use common sense. The interviewers don't want to know that you have 2 sisters, 3 brothers and a great aunt Gladys. All of the information you provide needs to BETTER your chances. You should give them only basic information such as where you studied your GCSEs, and expand more upon areas such as where you trained to teach and how this has affected your outlook.

Use the box on the following page to write out your response to this question. Once you've done that, compare your answer with our sample response underneath.

<u>Sample Response</u>

'I am a confident, enthusiastic and responsible person, with a genuine passion and desire for improving the education of young people. I myself have a great standard of education, and achieved high GCSE grades, A-Levels, undergrad and postgrad marks in my subject field – English Literature. I recently completed my PGCE teacher training, and now I am ready to move into the world of work.

I believe that I am a great fit for a career as a teacher, and for your school. As a result of my PGCE training, I have picked up large amounts of experience in different school settings; including working in a special school for children with behavioural difficulties, and in various secondary institutions. I have also worked part-time as an English tutor for young people, on and off, for several years. All of this has taught me a great deal about how to conduct myself with integrity and professionalism, and how to impart my wisdom on others.

I've conducted thorough research into your school, and was hugely impressed by what I have discovered. The learning style, ethos and range of extra-curricular activities that you offer are extremely appealing to me. I want to teach children that learning doesn't have to be limited to the school environment; it can be something that they enjoy doing after school is finished. I believe that I am the right person to demonstrate this.'

Q2. How many different age groups have you worked with? Tell us about your experiences with these.

This is a good question for you, as it's almost impossible to give a wrong answer. All you need to do is give an honest recount of your experiences of working with different age brackets, and list some of the challenges you faced. You should try to be as detailed as possible, whilst demonstrating that you have picked up significant experience along the way. It's not a mistake here to tell the interviewers that you enjoyed working with one particular age group, as this could lead to you teaching within that bracket in the future.

Along with the above, it's also a good idea to use this question as a way of showing what you have learnt. You could give this in smaller subsections, '*I learnt this from this age bracket*' or even just as a wider conclusion, stating what you have learnt from all your experiences. Make sure you demonstrate your understanding of the fact that each age bracket requires different learning strategies and approaches.

Overall, the key to answering this question is in showing the interviewers that you are an experienced and capable individual, who would excel working with any group of students.

Use the box on the following page to write out your response to this question. Once you've done that, compare your answer with our sample response underneath.

<u>Sample Response</u>

'So far in my teaching career, I have had experience with a large number of different age brackets.

In my previous school I was directly involved in the teaching of Years 1 and 2, and also worked as a parent intermediary. This essentially meant that if parents of students in that age bracket had any concerns, they could contact me to arrange a meeting. This enabled me to build close relationships with the parents of pupils in my year groups, and with the pupils themselves. Part of this role also involved producing learning initiatives for selected students in the age bracket, who were struggling. This was a really engaging position which gave me a great deal of responsibility. I learned how to communicate on a non-teacher basis with a wide range of pupils, and their parents. The latter was a new and challenging experience for me. This is a role that taught me a great deal about the value of organisation and tailoring learning for specific students.

Prior to that position, I worked in a local secondary school – teaching English. I taught across a wide range of age brackets during my time at this school, with the youngest being Year 7 and the oldest being Year 12. I was at this school for five years, during which time I learned an enormous amount. This was my first real teaching position post PGCE, and therefore I went into the role with limited experience. I would argue that my experiences at this school have shaped me as a teacher. While the PGCE and initial observation lessons provided me with my first real introduction into the world of teaching, it was this job which really gave me the tools for success. It taught me responsibility and leadership. It gave me sustained confidence in myself, that I am a good teacher and that I can stand up in front of a class and lead by example.

More than anything however, this role taught me the huge difference between what is required for different age groups in schools. I went into the job expecting to take the same teaching approach/style to all of my lessons; but very quickly discovered that this wouldn't work. I have learned that different age groups require a very different approach to learning, and the sheer importance of flexibility when teaching. Without this quality, I don't believe I could have succeeded in the role.'

Q3. What skills do you have which distinguish you from other candidates?

This is a great question, and one that directly invites you to sell yourself. So, sell yourself! Another way of wording this could be: 'what are your biggest strengths?' The interviewer isn't actually looking for you to tell them why they shouldn't hire other candidates, or for special qualities that they've never encountered before. Let's be honest, your answers and those of your competitors are probably going to overlap. Yes, everybody has different skills but unless you can juggle whilst standing on one leg, it will be extremely hard for you to show the interviewer something completely new (not that this would be relevant to the job role!) No, when answering this question you need to show how and why your skills and qualities are extensive enough for the position. The best way to do this is to demonstrate your skills via past examples.

In your examples you should show that you have the ability to take things further and go the extra mile. This is what will distinguish you from the other candidates, and help you nail the answer to this question.

Be specific about what you did and how you acted, but remember that you also need to demonstrate 2 or 3 strengths in this answer. This is a great example of where planning prior to the interview will set you apart from the crowd.

Use the box on the following page to write out your response to this question. Once you've done that, compare your answer with our sample response underneath.

Sample Response

'Great question. I believe that I have a number of qualities which set me apart from the crowd, and make me an ideal candidate to work in your school.

Firstly, there is my level of teaching experience. While it's true that I have only just finished my PGCE, I feel that the level of experience I picked up before and during this course is unique. Throughout my course, and prior to this, I went to great lengths to gain extra experience on top of what I was already doing. Coupled with a rigorous course, which involved numerous placements in school settings, I have also gone out of my way to gain other experience in schools.

I spent extra time almost every single week in my school placements; wherever possible, learning from the staff and assisting students with extra-curricular learning activities. I assisted with both the Creative Writing and after-school English clubs, which were designed to help students improve the quality of their grammar and writing. Both of these assignments gave me a chance to interact on a one-to-one basis with students, and further my teaching skills. I found this extremely rewarding and believe it has greatly enhanced my teaching skills.

Secondly, there is my subject expertise. As someone with a PHD in English Literature, I believe that I am fantastically placed to deliver the curriculum material to your students. Teachers are role models, and who better to act as a role model than someone who has achieved top level marks from GCSE onwards? I feel that my age benefits me in this respect. As someone who is young and near fresh out of university, I will have no problem identifying and bonding with my students. For me, this is an essential part of successful teaching.

Finally, I firmly believe that my passion and drive to succeed in this role is unrivalled. I'm sure you'll hear the same thing from other candidates, but I believe that my experience and history of taking initiative backs this up. I have always gone out of my way to excel and improve myself, and I would take the same attitude with this position.'

Q4. Where do you see yourself in ten years' time?

This is a question that you'll often be asked at interviews, and is designed to test your ambition. Again, this is a question where it's more important not to get the answer wrong, than it is to get it right. You should avoid:

- Telling the interviewer that you have no idea. This will tell them that you lack ambition. It also shows that you have not prepared for your interview, which will obviously reflect poorly on your application. You need to show the interviewers that you have the drive and ambition to succeed.

- Telling the interviewer something unrealistic. For example, informing them that you see yourself as being the principal of the school in 10 years' time, or that you'll be their boss. This will make you come across as arrogant and conceited, and will be extremely damaging to your application.

So, how should you answer? The answer is very simple. Just give a level and liberal response which clearly incorporates the expectations of a teacher. Reasonable aims such as having your students achieving top marks, helping the school to exceed OFSTED expectations or even being head of the department; will go a long way to securing the position you are interviewing for.

Use the box on the following page to write out your response to this question. Once you've done that, compare your answer with our sample response underneath.

<u>Sample Response</u>

'*I'm quite an ambitious person, and I want to do my absolute best, and to this end I have several long-term goals.*

Firstly, I'd like to be with this school for a substantial amount of time. By this I mean several years at the very least. I see this as a long-term position and I want to make my mark on this school in a positive way.

To add to this, just as any teacher would, the aim in 10 years would be to have all of my students achieving the highest grades that they possibly can. I'm realistic, and I know that not every student will achieve straight As, but as teachers we can only be satisfied if we know that we have done everything possible to aid them in this endeavour.

Finally, along with teaching, I'd like to be benefitting the school. This would extend to helping the school achieve outstanding OFSTED results, and participating in a wide range of extra-curricular learning activities. My ultimate goal in 10 years' time would be to become the head of the English department.'

Q5. What are the challenges currently facing teachers of your subject today, and how do you intend to deal with these?

Another subject-focused question, this ties in with the previous, in that the interviewer is asking you to focus specifically on what the needs of the subject are.

If you've conducted your teacher training, then you should have a good idea of the challenges that you'll face in teaching the subject. Elements such as curriculum material, students' attitudes towards the subject and public perception should all be taken into account.

This question doesn't just want you to reel off the problems either. You need to show that you have thought about long-term solutions in order to resolve these issues. This is a great opportunity for you, as it gives you a chance to demonstrate your capacity for creative thinking, as well as your competency as a teacher. If you want to produce a really good answer, you could even give the interviewer an example of how you have resolved a problem like this before.

Use the box on the following page to write out your response to this question. Once you've done that, compare your answer with our sample response underneath.

Sample Response

'There are a great number of issues facing present day English teachers, but I am confident that I am well placed to deal with these.

Firstly, I believe we are at something of a crossroads in terms of reading vs technology. While it's true that better technology (such as Kindle) has actually increased the capacity for students to read, this doesn't necessarily mean that they are doing it. From my experience, students would rather use devices such as these to browse the Internet and play games, as opposed to reading books. This means that such technology is acting more as a distraction than a tool for learning. Don't get me wrong, I'm all for technology and modernising, but ultimately my job as an English teacher is to encourage students to read. To resolve this, we need to persuade students that technology can be an exciting tool for learning, and not just as a break from their studies. One way that I tackled this during my PGCE placement was to try and use interactive, digital-based lessons as much as possible. Instead of having students sitting at their desks reading from a book, I booked out an IT suite at the school and had them read the books from their screens. I found that this had a positive impact on their learning and the class seemed to show a better retention rate than they would have done if I had simply handed them a book.

Secondly, another issue that I have found is to do with preconceptions surrounding the subject itself. Based on my interactions with pupils and parents alike, I have discovered that there is a worrying degree of misunderstanding of what English Literature involves and how it impacts upon students' lives. I think this is best summed up by an example of an interaction that I had with a student in one of my PGCE classes. After questioning the student on why he was misbehaving, I was informed that he thought the subject was 'pointless' and that critically analysing texts wouldn't help him in life. I then proceeded to open a book and point out several different themes, before linking them to potential areas in his life that they might impact upon. This apparently made the student think, and following this meeting, he became far more engaged in the lessons. As English teachers, it is our duty to spread awareness and defeat ignorance, the latter being a plague upon any subject.

Finally, there is the challenge of asking students to look beyond the text. This is not just an English teacher challenge, but one that is apparent across all subjects. In order to amend the media perception of the schooling system as a means of programming exam answers into students, we must be able to get more out of our students. We need to teach them to think with an open mind, produce ideas for themselves and apply these skills in real-world situations. It is our duty to show the world that school is not just a results-orientated machine, but a place where children will grow and develop into responsible and mature adults.'

Q6. What is your biggest weakness?

This is a very common interview question, yet still catches a large number of people out. When conducting your interview preparation, make sure you plan for this question. This is one of the questions where it's more important not to get the answer wrong, than it is to get the answer right.

<u>There are two things to avoid here:</u>

- Firstly, don't tell the interviewer that you have no weaknesses. This is a lie, and the interviewers will know it. You'll come across as dishonest, or arrogant and lacking self-awareness. Teachers should be constantly trying to improve their practice, and therefore telling the interviewer that you have nothing to improve will act as a warning sign for them.

- Secondly, don't tell the interviewer that you have weaknesses which will significantly infringe on your ability to do the job. For example, telling them that you have extremely poor organisational skills or struggle to impart wisdom. Obviously, this wouldn't be a wise thing to do, as it would immediately weaken your application in comparison to other candidates.

So, how do you answer this question? It's actually very simple. When answering the 'biggest weakness' question, you just need to take something still related to the job, and turn this into a positive. For example, you could tell the interviewer that talking in front of people makes you quite nervous, but that you are working on this and have put yourself in lots of public-speaking situations, in hope to overcome these fears.

The most popular answer to this question is undoubtedly to tell the interviewer that you are a perfectionist, who sometimes struggles to delegate. However, it's worth pointing out that the interviewers will probably have heard this answer hundreds of times before. This devalues the response, so think carefully before you use it.

Use the box on the following page to write out your response to this question. Once you've done that, compare your answer with our sample response underneath.

<u>Sample Response</u>

'That's a tough one! I would say that my biggest weakness is that I do sometimes get nervous talking in front of people. However, this is something that I have worked hard on and it's no longer a big issue for me. In the past, I let this impact upon my performance whilst teaching and it held me back. Through significant practice, and the help of my PGCE mentors, I have overcome this issue and now feel much more confident in leading classes.

After suffering this issue on a number of occasions at the start of my PGCE, I decided to take immediate action. I signed up for an exterior 'presentation skills' club within my local community, which trained attendants to become exceptional public speakers. The end result of this was not only that I improved my teaching ability tenfold, but I also ended up giving a number of speeches at the golf club where I worked part time (during weekends). All of this has contributed to my ability to teach in a clear and confident manner.

I fully understand that it's essential to, at the very least, project an image of confidence to your students. This is a fundamental aspect of good leadership. If you want students to follow your lead, then you need them to believe in you. How can they believe in you if you don't believe in yourself?'

Q7. If you had to pick one quality, what do you think is the most important asset for a teacher to have?

To answer this question, you'll need to have a good knowledge of the teaching core competencies. These have been provided to you at the start of the book, so make sure you study these carefully beforehand.

You need to give a thorough answer to this question, explaining exactly why the quality is important and how it's relevant to the school environment. A good answer to this won't just explain how and why the quality is important, but will also list an example of when you have demonstrated this quality. As this isn't a competency-based question, you don't need to go into an extensive detail, but make sure you clearly convey how you used the quality in the context of teaching.

Use the box on the following page to write out your response to this question. Once you've done that, compare your answer with our sample response underneath.

Sample Response

'In my opinion, the most important quality that a teacher can have is good organisation. There are many reasons for this.

Firstly, it's important to recognise that good organisation incorporates a huge range of other qualities. These include the fundamentals such as time management and lesson planning. Organisation brings out the best in all of the other qualities which are fundamental to succeeding as a teacher, and therefore this is a skill which helps a great deal.

Secondly, organisation is the key skill required to succeed in the chaotic school environment. I fully understand that teachers have a difficult and stressful job, which involves a significant amount of planning time and a strong need for self-discipline.

Based on my experience, the most common complaint that I have heard from other teachers is that they don't have enough time in the day to complete all of their tasks. I also know that it's extremely hard to manage lessons, with misbehaviour or overrunning discussions eating into your planned time. Good organisation will go a long way to fixing this.

Overall, I feel that organisation is absolutely essential. As teachers, it is our duty to stay organised and focused, in turn minimising the stress of the job. This will help us to get the best out of ourselves, and our students.'

Q8. Why have you applied to this school, and what do you know about us?

Before you attend any interview, it's essential that you prepare carefully. A big part of this preparation means researching the school in great detail. Schools are looking to hire someone who has a genuine interest in their institution and learning ethos, not just candidates who are applying to every single job that comes up. They want to hire someone who cares about their cause. By showing the school that you have conducted research into both the position and the institution, you will immediately indicate that you do care, and are not just looking for any old teaching job.

Regardless of the position to which you are applying, you will need to show potential employers that you are enthusiastic and interested. Demonstrating that you have researched the school, and that you have the same values, ethos and interests as them, will go a long way to securing the position.

Remember that you don't need to go overboard when answering this question. Don't lie or exaggerate. For example, telling the school that they are the best school in the entire country, or extending lavish praise to areas in which they don't particularly excel, will come across as insincere. This will be extremely transparent to the interviewer. If you've researched properly, you'll have a good idea of which areas the school are strongest in, so focus on these!

Another thing to look out for when you are researching schools is their learning ethos. In simple terms, this refers to the values and principles of the school. For example, the school might be particularly dedicated to teaching IT skills to underprivileged children. Alternatively, in a general sense, they might be dedicated to reinforcing the idea of university as a positive next step. Write down a list of these aims and values and then compare them with your own qualities and goals. You can use this to great effect in your interview answer.

Finally, make sure you list something specific or appealing about the responsibilities and job description, which makes it worthwhile for you.

Use the box on the following page to write out your response to this question. Once you've done that, compare your answer with our sample response underneath.

<u>Sample Response</u>

'I applied for a position at this school for a number of reasons. Through extensive research, I have discovered that there are a great number of things which I admire about your school; and in turn I feel that I would provide a fantastic service to both you and your students.

Firstly, I believe that the learning ethos of your school bears extremely close resemblance to my own. I know that this school is really passionate about promoting extra-curricular learning, and has a high percentage of students who go on to pursue a university degree.

Along with promoting the value of education in general, these are both areas which I am extremely passionate about. During my PGCE placements, I made a conscious effort to take part in as many extra-curricular learning activities as I could. I wanted to engage myself in the school environment and get to know the students.

Furthermore, as someone who has been to university and reaped the enormous benefits, I believe I'm in a fantastic position to promote this to students. I strongly believe in the value of further education, and improving one's skillset and knowledge. It is my belief that once you start to promote this message to students, you'll see an immediate improvement in results. Persuading children to think long-term is one of the greatest challenges of being a teacher, but I believe I am well placed to meet this challenge.

Finally, I've looked at the curriculum that English teachers in your school will deliver to students, and am delighted to say that I believe the list is perfect for me. I've covered every single one of the topics either during my degree or at A-Level and GCSE. With a quick refresh, I'd be ready to teach these subjects to anyone, at any time! Having spoken to one of the teachers in your department, to discuss the responsibilities that your staff members hold, I can safely say that I am more than up for the task.'

Q9. How would you ensure that you are a great teacher?

To be a great teacher, you must be someone who is prepared to go above and beyond what would generally be expected, in order to make things better for your students. You don't need to just do 'a good job' but you need to be absolutely great at supporting, mentoring and teaching your students.

Your lessons need to be fun, interactive, and make learning enjoyable.

Not only do you need to achieve good results, but you need to be able to do this whilst keeping the students in your class engaged in the subject, and informed on how the subject matters in the wider context. A good teacher teaches students; a great teacher makes them want to learn.

Use the box on the following page to write out your response to this question. Once you've done that, compare your answer with our sample response underneath.

<u>Sample Response</u>

'There are plenty of ways that I would ensure I was a great teacher.

A great teacher is someone who endeavours to try their hardest with their students. They dedicate their time, effort and support to their class and do their utmost to increase interest in the subject material. They are always on hand to help their students when they need it. A great teacher doesn't just do all these things though; they absolutely exceed all expectations in all of these areas.

As teachers, we should be more than just educators, or even mentors. Our goal should be for our students to genuinely enjoy the subject material, and to take their own initiative in learning it for themselves. It should be for us to persuade students that the subject is worth pursuing outside or after their school education is finished. We need to teach students that university is a positive step, and that lessons taught at school prepare students for their future.

A great teacher is someone who can persuade their students to invest high levels of passion and dedication in their subject.'

Q10. Tell me about one experience that you've had which changed your outlook on teaching.

During the 'getting to know you' stage of the interview, you can expect to be asked at least one question based around your personal experiences of teaching. This isn't a question which requires you to answer with core competencies, unlike the actual experience side of the interview, but it will provide the interviewers with an insight into what drives and motivates you, and how you deal with the natural pressures of teaching.

When answering this question, make sure you answer with as much clarity and structure as possible. You should give a clear run-through of the experience, listing exactly what happened, how it changed your outlook and why it impacted you in the way that it did.

Clearly explain the emotional consequences of this experience and how they changed you. Make sure you choose a positive example/ experience that improved or changed you in a good way.

Use the box on the following page to write out your response to this question. Once you've done that, compare your answer with our sample response underneath.

Sample Response

'Early on in my PGCE course, I was given a placement in a local school. I was assigned to work with a Year 8 English group, observing and assisting the teacher with her lessons.

The class in question was fairly rowdy and difficult to manage. During group work, I noticed one of the students sitting alone. The student in question had a disability, and unfortunately was being ignored by his classmates as a result. I pointed this out to the teacher, who encouraged me to go and sit with the student and try to help him.

After a few minutes of discussing with the student, the teacher came and sat down next to us, to make a 3 person group. I was really impressed by the way she comforted the individual; who was clearly upset about being ignored by the rest of the class. It was inspiring to see her manage such a difficult situation, and treat the student with respect, just as she would have with any other pupil.

One of the things that this experience taught me is that teachers are not just there to help students learn the subject matter. They are also role models and guardian figures, who are there to provide support and encouragement to students. Teachers can have a really significant impact on a student's life. On this occasion, by behaving the way that she did, the teacher in my lesson demonstrated a belief in fairness and equality; and showed the student that his disability was not something that should hold him back.

I came away from this experience feeling extremely positive and wanting to have the same impact on my students' lives. I strongly believe in equality, and feel that it's essential to demonstrate this at all times in the classroom environment.'

Q11. Would you consider yourself a team player, or do you prefer working alone?

Read the above question carefully. On the face of it, it might seem like the interviewer is giving you a straight choice between two options; but in reality the best way to answer this is to sidestep the choice and tell them that you like to do both! The reason for this is that teaching is about both elements.

On the one hand, when you are hired by the school, you are being granted a place in their wider team. You'll be working alongside other teachers, admin staff, student support services and others to ensure that the pupils at the school are being treated safely and fairly. Your wider objective is student wellbeing. In a school that is packed full of students, this is extremely hard to get right, so it's essential that staff are working in close conjunction with each other. This is especially important when it comes to working with other members of your learning department. As experts in the field, it goes without saying that you'll need to work together to provide the best teaching experience for your students. By exchanging tips and information, you can guarantee that your teaching methods are at their best possible standards.

Teaching is often a one-person job. Unless you are working with a teaching or learning assistant, ultimately you are on your own at the front of the class; and this is the same when it comes to lesson planning, marking, etc. This all involves a huge amount of responsibility and self-belief. You can't be a teacher if you can't work on your own. Your students are your responsibility: it is your job to get them to a subject level where they can achieve good grades and grow as individuals.

Use the box on the following page to write out your response to this question. Once you've done that, compare your answer with our sample response underneath.

Sample Response

'I am actually someone who is very happy to do both. I recognise the benefits of working in a team and working alone, both of which are necessary for teachers.

I'm a great team player, and have demonstrated this on a huge number of occasions. Throughout my career, I've worked within, and led, many different teams to success. I've done this in a number of different fields including in a restaurant, in an admin team and even during my PGCE; so I believe that I have a fantastic grasp of what teamwork involves and how a team should be run and managed. I know that teamwork is essential for teachers, as they'll be working in the wider school team, especially in their chosen department. It's imperative that, as teachers, we are able to communicate effectively – not just to our students, but to the rest of the staff who ultimately have the same aim as you! By working as part of a team, we can guarantee that no student is left wanting, and we are able to do our utmost to ensure that every child goes home happy at the end of the day. Good teamwork leads to great grades!

On the other hand, I am also very capable and happy to work on my own. I've got great drive and am always looking to take the initiative. At the end of the day, all of the teamwork that goes into working at a school means nothing if you can't stand up at the front of the class, on your own, and deliver a great lesson. This extends to lesson planning, marking and subject knowledge, too. The wider school team provides a fantastic support base for teachers, and works to safeguard the wellbeing of students, but the actual teaching element of the job is an individual task. This is something I greatly look forward to.'

Q12. If you aren't successful today, what will be your next step?

This is another trick question, so think carefully about your response before answering. You might look at this and think that you need to show the interviewer how devastated you'll be, but this is a risky strategy. Yes it's true that you should show the interviewer that you care about working for them, but this question is asked to test your resolve and motivation for becoming a teacher. With this in mind, a bad response would be to tell the interviewer that if you can't teach at this school, then you don't want to teach at all. This would show a lack of drive and dedication. Essentially, you need to show that while you'd still be highly disappointed not to have received the job, this wouldn't deter you from trying to become a teacher.

Remember that the best teachers are people who never give up when faced with adversity. If being rejected by an interviewer is enough to deter you from teaching, then you certainly won't be able to handle a class full of (sometimes uncouth) children!

Use the box on the following page to write out your response to this question. Once you've done that, compare your answer with our sample response underneath.

<u>Sample Response</u>

'If I was rejected from this job, then I would obviously be highly disappointed. I see this as an ideal place for me to work and believe that I'd be a fantastic addition to your team.

However, this would not deter me from becoming a teacher. I am determined to make a success of myself in this career and would continue applying to schools. I really believe that I would make a fantastic teacher.

I am experienced, motivated and passionate about this endeavour, and I have a fantastic depth of knowledge in the subject. I have no doubt that I will find a position that is suitable for me and will become a great teacher.'

Q13. Describe your teaching style.

There is no wrong answer to this question, although ideally you need to make your teaching style sound like something worth investing in. The interviewers aren't expecting to hear a revolutionary response here, or for you to give them something a style they've never heard of before.

Steer away from answers such as 'I'm very big on discipline' because these will just flash warning signs for the interviewer. Better responses to this question will incorporate ideas such as group work, exercises and class engagement. You'll need to demonstrate capability of being flexible and recognise when a different teaching style is appropriate for the lesson in question.

Use the box on the following page to write out your response to this question. Once you've done that, compare your answer with our sample response underneath.

Sample Response

'I would say that my teaching style is primarily centred on class engagement. They need to engage with the subject material that is being taught, and this can be tricky sometimes, because not everyone likes the same things. I try to adapt my teaching style in order to cater for everyone and make the material as interesting as possible. I like to use group exercises, colourful PowerPoint slides and even videos to demonstrate my learning points. I believe that this is something which increases student interest significantly, and from my experience, leads to a better learning experience overall. I'm very keen to take a 'digital approach' to learning, and believe that modernising the classroom is very important. I'm also extremely focused on time management, and endeavour to make sure that my lesson is interactive and that my pupils' retention rate remains from beginning to end.

Having said all of that, I am a very flexible person and am completely prepared to change up my style when it is required. I understand that not all classes can be run in the above way, and sometimes a more structured, disciplined approach is required. While I'm not a teacher who students will find 'scary', I'm more than capable of laying down the law in lessons; throughout my PGCE I managed my classes extremely effectively.

Whether I'm using fun exercises or simply speaking to the group; I always ensure that the class I am teaching are taking in the information in the right way, and are behaving themselves, to ensure maximum learning potential.'

Q14. Would you say that you are someone who can handle criticism?

This is fairly similar to Q12, in that the interviewers are trying to test your motivation and ability to survive in the school environment. The answer to this question is yes, you are absolutely someone who can handle criticism, and take it on board constructively. This is important for two reasons:

Firstly, you'll be expected to work with other teachers in your department. This means exchanging ideas, views and tips on teaching. It is almost inevitable that there will be teachers in the department who are more senior than you; who have been teaching for a great number of years. While this doesn't mean that they are always right, you should always be looking to learn from them. Constructive criticism is something that should be welcomed, considered and used in order to improve your teaching practice.

Secondly, your students! Teaching isn't easy, and sometimes children can be fairly spiteful or personal towards you. As a teacher, it's important that you don't take this personally or let it damage your practice. Remember that they are just children; as the teacher it's your job to show them that behaviour like this is unacceptable and teach right from wrong. On the other hand, some students will actually provide you with useful critical feedback. Teaching is all about listening. With this in mind, if a student (or even a whole class) tells you that they are struggling to work with your current style, then you need to consider changing it up.

Use the box on the following page to write out your response to this question. Once you've done that, compare your answer with our sample response underneath.

<u>Sample Response</u>

'I would say that I am someone who is highly capable of taking on board constructive criticism, and using it to improve my teaching practice. As a new teacher, I'm extremely eager to learn, and this means that I would welcome any feedback from teachers at your school on my style. I believe that my time at university and during the PGCE has really enhanced my ability to take criticism constructively and appreciate the opinions of others.

Along with this, I'm also capable of brushing off criticism which might not be so constructive. For example, when teaching children or adolescents, I'm aware that I'll receive some comments from students which they don't really mean. I'm resilient and thick-skinned enough not to let this bother me, and have already had first-hand experience of dealing with this in a school. Despite this, I am also receptive enough to recognise when students' criticism should be taken seriously. For example, if a class was telling me that the lesson or learning style was not helping them, I'd endeavour to change things up for the good of the class.

Overall, I believe I'm a very flexible and reasonable person, who appreciates the need for feedback and criticism. The aim of every teacher should be to improve, and we can only do this by listening to and taking on board the feedback of other professionals and our students.'

Q15. Why do you believe that AFL is important?

AFL stands for *'Assessment For Learning'*. This is a popular teaching theory/strategy, which incorporates feedback into the learning process. Students actively engage in the learning process and using the feedback, take active steps to get to where they want to be and the level they want to reach.

If you have completed your teacher training, then you'll be highly familiar with the 5 critical AFL steps:

1. Questioning.

This allows a student to work out which level they are currently performing at.

2. Feedback.

This gives the teacher a chance to provide students with feedback on how they can improve their current performance.

3. Example Success.

This means that students understand what a successful piece of work looks like, before completing their own.

4. Independent Assessment.

This allows students to take part in peer-to-peer assessment or self-assessment.

5. Performance Assessment.

This allows students to use their own work or submissions/exams or essays, to improve their current performance.

Your response to this question needs to focus on one particular element of AFL, and why you believe it's essential. It's common to get asked at least one theory-based question in the teaching interview, so make sure you brush up beforehand!

Use the box on the following page to write out your response to this question. Once you've done that, compare your answer with our sample response underneath.

Sample Response

'Throughout my PGCE I have learned that AFL is extremely important. Not only does it provide teachers with a structural framework for learning, but it also provides students with clear guidelines on how to improve.

For me, the biggest advocate for AFL is that it helps students to become so much more active in their own learning. In some ways, it actually helps them to start thinking like a teacher and taking real initiative in their own performance.

Teaching has improved significantly over the last decade. It's no longer about students sitting in a lesson being dictated to. AFL gets pupils to really think about what level they are currently at, how their performance can change this, and how they can improve their performance to increase achievement. I think this is fantastic!

With the help of strategies such as AFL, teaching has become so much more than a one-way street, and it's really satisfying as a teacher to watch your students take responsibility and initiative for their learning.'

Q16. What is it about this subject in particular, that makes you want to teach it?

In this question, the interviewers are looking to assess your level of commitment to the subject itself. Even if you've taken a year-long PGCE course, the school still knows something that you don't – teaching long-term is extremely hard work! It's important that they are hiring a member of staff who is actually dedicated to their subject area, and isn't just teaching it purely because they know it or are good at it. You might have fantastic school and degree marks, but that doesn't necessarily mean that you enjoy your particular subject, and it doesn't mean you have the capacity to teach it long term. After a year or two, you might become disillusioned or bored, and what happens then? Either you leave, or your capacity to teach will be reduced. This is why it's essential for schools to assess your subject knowledge and dedication before they hire you.

If you are truly interested in the subject, then great, now is the chance to show the interviewers why. This should be easy. List the areas in which you are the most interested, tell them about research papers that you have read and explain why you believe the subject is important in the wider context. The latter is particularly important. It's well known that the education system is under increasing pressure, from those who claim that schools are only interested in generating good test scores from their students, and not actually in teaching them. Schools are keen to shake this reputation, and the best way for them to do so is to recruit teachers who can show their students why the subject really matters. School isn't just about teaching basic subject knowledge; it's about imparting real world skills and life lessons through the subject material.

Use the box on the following page to write out your response to this question. Once you've done that, compare your answer with our sample response underneath.

<u>Sample Response</u>

'Having taken English to postgraduate level, and taught it during my PGCE, it is safe to say that I'm very passionate about the subject. There are a number of reasons for this:

Firstly, it goes without saying that English is an essential subject. Basic writing and reading are a fundamental aspect of everyday life, and every child should have the right of access to these skills. Without deriding other subjects, it is my view that basic English is the most important lesson that can be taught in the school environment. It is this subject that forms the building blocks for all other subjects too, and therefore illustrates how significant English is to our National Curriculum.

Secondly, moving away from basic English, I believe that encouraging students to read and analyse is extremely important. By doing this we are increasing their ability to think for themselves and broadening the spectrum of their imagination. Good ideas come from those who have been taught how to appreciate the ideas of others, not those who are ignorant and single-minded. English Literature introduces children to a wide range of viewpoints and perspectives, and often encourages them to think outside of the box, or look deeper for underlying meanings. It's about considering what's beneath the surface of a text, and I believe this is something that will be extremely important in their everyday lives. Students learn about love, history, war and justice and other sophisticated themes, which ultimately serve to broaden their minds.

Thirdly, in conjunction with the above, I believe that English Literature teaches us about more than just literary themes. It teaches us about ourselves. It is a study of human nature, through literature, and how humans and the English language have developed over time. This is a subject that produces mature, well-rounded and creative-thinking students, and that is very important in today's society.'

Q17. What is your personal policy on bullying?

Before hiring you, it's important that the interviewers can establish that you meet the school values and expectations. It is a requirement for any school to have a no-tolerance policy on bullying, so your answer here should be fairly simple. Bullying is not acceptable under any circumstances. Answers such as 'it builds character' will end the interview pretty fast.

It's essential that schools are doing their utmost to promote equality, fairness and unity amongst their students. As a teacher, you play a central role in delivering this expectation, so make sure you demonstrate your sheer no-tolerance towards bullying in any form.

Use the box on the following page to write out your response to this question. Once you've done that, compare your answer with our sample response underneath.

<u>Sample Response</u>

'Bullying is absolutely unacceptable, and I take a no-tolerance approach to it. Every single student should come to school with the expectation that they will be treated fairly, equally and with respect; not just from teachers but from their peers, too. As teachers, I fully understand that we have a leading part to play in the fight against bullying, and to this end I would do my utmost to ensure that it does not take place.

The aim of the school should be to create a warm and inviting atmosphere, and to produce students who are vigilant, decent and without fear. Only by showing students that bullying and discrimination will not be tolerated, can we achieve this.'

Q18. Why do you want to leave your current position?

This is a tricky question, and you need to think carefully about your response. Some people might be inclined to launch full blown into a tirade about their current employer, why they are unhappy in their job and reel off the many things they don't like. This is a big mistake. You can be honest, but you need to maintain your professionalism and don't give inappropriate details. It's also a mistake to tell them that you are leaving because of differences with management or disputes. This will flash warning signs to the interviewer. Even if you are in the right, don't forget that they won't know the full situation. All it will do is show that you are someone who is potentially disagreeable and difficult to work with. You should do your utmost to make your previous employer sound positive. Think about it like this: if you did get this job and then left after a few years, would the employer want you to say positive things about them? Of course they would. A person who is in the habit of discrediting their former employers is an unattractive proposition for new employers.

Finally, avoid telling the interviewers that you are leaving because 'you want a higher salary'. This might well be the case, but it will make you look money motivated and this is never a good thing.

So, what should you say? The answer is actually fairly simple. You just need to tell the interviewer that you feel you have achieved all that you can in your current position, and that you are looking for a new challenge. This shows drive, enthusiasm and a desire to achieve bigger and better things. It demonstrates that you are ambitious and looking to succeed at their school.

Use the box on the following page to write out your response to this question. Once you've done that, compare your answer with our sample response underneath.

<u>Sample Response</u>

'I'm really grateful for all of the opportunities I have been given in my current position, and I have learned so much from this job. My employers have been fantastic and I'm so happy to have worked where I have for the past few years. However, it's time to move on.

I feel that I have achieved all that I can in this position, and it is no longer satisfying the ambitious side of my personality which longs to achieve bigger and better things. I don't feel challenged by this role anymore, which was initially so rewarding. I feel that moving on is the right thing to do.

I strongly believe that the role I am applying for today is absolutely perfect for me, not just in terms of my personality but in terms of the challenges I will encounter. It will more than satisfy my desire to achieve and accomplish things, in a fresh and exciting environment, and I am hugely excited to have the opportunity. In particular, I am excited to have the chance to work within an English department that is as highly regarded as yours, and learn from the established professionals within the team.'

Q19. Give me the top 3 rules that you expect your students to follow in the classroom, and tell me why these are important to you.

During your interview you can always expect to have, at the very least, one question based on classroom management.

The rules that a teacher sets out for their class are very important, and will tell the interviewers a lot about your style of teaching. The key to answering this is to find a safe balance. For example, answers such as 'no talking whatsoever' won't impress the interviewers. You need to set realistic expectations of the group. Even though it might be frustrating, all teachers experience background chatter at some point. You are teaching a class full of children; this is completely normal. Don't be too strict, or you'll risk putting off the interviewers. Similarly, you should avoid being too lax. For example, telling the interviewers that your number one rule is 'to always have fun in the classroom'. In principle this might sound good, and it's admirable to keep your students engaged, but this should never come at the expense of order and control.

Better answers to this question will take a liberal but authoritative approach to classroom management. Rules such as 'putting your hand up before speaking,' 'always using manners,' 'making sure you ask if you don't understand,' or 'no swinging on chairs' will demonstrate that you are a reasonable and sensible teacher.

Use the box on the following page to write out your response to this question. Once you've done that, compare your answer with our sample response underneath.

<u>Sample Response</u>

'*I always have three main rules that I expect to be followed in my classrooms. These are:*

-No swinging on chairs. This is a personal paranoia of mine, and I want the students in my classroom to be safe. When I was a student, I witnessed a classmate crack their head open after swinging on a chair (despite repeated warnings). It's now firmly ingrained in me that I don't want this happening in my classroom! Student welfare should be our number one priority.

-Putting your hand up before speaking. This coincides with having good manners. I'm very strict on this rule, and I always found university seminars quite difficult as a result! I've always been taught to put my hand up before speaking. A failure to do so leads to everyone speaking out of turn and the class will lose structure and focus as a result. Therefore, I believe this is really important.

-Having respect for your classmates. I won't tolerate nastiness in my classrooms, and I will never accept bullying in any way, shape or form. Not only is bullying unacceptable, but I also believe that classes are far more likely to run in a smooth and orderly fashion if students are working in conjunction with each other, and are not at each other's throats.'

> **Q20. How do you feel about using the Internet as an educational tool?**

You should expect to hear at least one question based around modern teaching methods during your interview, and it's likely that this question or its answer will involve the Internet in some capacity. The best answer to this will give a balanced approach.

Telling the interviewers that you are totally against using the Internet as a teaching tool will make you seem out of touch. However, if you do praise the Internet as a means of learning, you also need to recognise/ identify the challenges of using it. Problems such as the Internet being an easy distraction from work, inappropriate websites and even worries over screen time could factor into your answer. Remember that schools are trying to modernise, and keep up-to-date, in order to maximise the learning experience for their pupils. If you want to be really technical, you could even make reference to specific programmes such as iTALC, which allow for a controlled ICT based learning experience.

Use the box on the following page to write out your response to this question. Once you've done that, compare your answer with our sample response underneath.

<u>Sample Response</u>

'I believe that it's really important to get pupils using the Internet in school, and I'm a huge advocate of implementing modern technology as a learning device. The Internet is a really important educational tool, and showing them how to use this for research and learning purposes will really benefit students' long-term educational future.

Despite this, I'm well aware of the challenges that this entails. There are a number of issues with the Internet. While it's a fantastic educational tool, it also has the capacity to massively distract pupils from the subject at hand, and the potential for misbehaviour is far greater where the Internet is involved. Secondly, we need to limit children's access to inappropriate content – which the Internet is chock full off. While the majority of schools now have strict filters in place, the unfortunate truth is that it's not possible to filter every last non-educational thing out there. This means that Internet lessons need to be conducted under strict supervision.

I am actually someone with a large amount of experience in this subject, as in my last position, I endeavoured to teach students using ICT as much as possible. Using software such as iTALC, I was able to maintain a strict control over my students' screens, and therefore maximise their learning potential. I would say I'm a technically adept person, who is proficient with using the Internet and different ICT-based systems. This means I can use the Internet and technology to full advantage during my lessons.'

Chapter 3
*Teacher Interview
(Part 2)*

Once you've got through the initial stages of the interview, you'll move onto stage 2. This is the competency-based section, and is much more difficult.

In this section of the interview, you'll be asked questions based around the core competencies listed at the start of this guide.

Before we look at how to use these competencies in your responses, let's have a quick recap of what the core competencies actually are.

Recap of Core Competencies

Listening. When placed in a class full of students, listening can be really difficult. It's imperative that teachers can listen to what their students are saying, in order to clarify what needs to be taught and in what manner. Teaching is all about your ability to impart wisdom through your responses, so if you can't listen, you can't teach!

Relationship Management. Relationship management is all about resolving conflict and disagreement, and encouraging a good relationship between the teacher and pupil. Not everyone can get along all of the time. As a teacher, it is your job to prevent this from escalating. You must be able to provide a calm, reasonable and objective support base.

Instructing. You must be able to give clear instructions, impart your wisdom in a way that your pupils will understand, and lead by example. It is no good having knowledge or behavioural skills if you have no idea of how to apply them in the teaching environment. The quality of your lessons will depend on your ability to deliver knowledge and information in a clear and concise fashion.

Organisation. Organisation will separate the good teachers from the bad, and many people would argue that this is actually the most important competency. Without good organisation, you will really struggle to succeed as a teacher, and this extends to time management. It's important that you can minimise stress as much as possible, in order to get the best out of yourself and your pupils.

Lesson Planning. Lesson planning will help you to stay organised, keep your classes on track, stay up-to-date with which classes still need to learn which material, and plan out every single day that you are teaching. Disruptions, overrunning discussions and slow students are all issues that will take away from the chances of your lessons running smoothly. Every minute that you have to waste asking the class to settle down, or behave, is a minute that you could have spent teaching.

Leadership. As the teacher, you are the leader of the class. Students will look up to you and require guidance. You will also act as the authority figure for the group; if your students respect you, you'll have a far easier time teaching them.

Professionalism. Teachers are there to provide an example for pupils, and therefore your students must be able to look up to you. This means that your behaviour both inside and outside of the classroom needs to be exemplary. Schools are extremely culturally diverse, and this means that everyone attending the school (staff or students) must be respectful of the differences between themselves and others, and treat every person that they meet in the same way. As a teacher, it's your job to enforce this, and show students the correct way to behave.

How To Use These Competencies

As we explained, you'll need to give examples of times when you have used these competencies in the past. These examples need to be extremely specific, detailed and positive about your role in the circumstances. At all times, you need to make sure that the interviewer is clear on how you went about resolving the situation, and how your actions had a direct, positive impact on the end result.

In order to do this, you will need to structure your responses. This is more difficult than it sounds. While you might be able to reel off a great story from the top of your head, it's not easy to formulate this into an interview response, especially when you factor nerves into the equation. If there is no structure, your response will be confusing to the interviewer. This will detract from the quality of your answer.

In order to add structure to your response, we suggest using the STAR method:

The STAR Method

The **STAR** method works most effectively when preparing responses to situational-type interview questions. It ensures that your responses to the interview questions follow a concise and logical sequence, making sure that you cover every possible area.

Situation – At the commencement of your response, you should explain what the situation was and who else was involved. This will be a relatively comprehensive explanation, so that the interviewer fully understands what it is that you are trying to explain.

Task – Next, explain what the task was. This will basically be an explanation of what had to be done and by whom.

Action – Then move on and explain what action you specifically took, and also what action other people took.

Result – Finally, explain what the result was following your actions. It is important to express that the result was achieved as a direct result of your actions.

Using this method not only shows your thought process for each response, but it allows you to take the time and think carefully about each step in order to formulate a clear, effective response.

The key to passing the second stage of the interview is to ensure that you can demonstrate the core competencies expected by the school, and combine this with knowledge of the school's policies and role expectations. If you can demonstrate that you meet these, you will have a great chance of passing.

Now, let's move onto the actual interview questions! Just as before, we've included a full sample response to each question, to assist you in your preparation! Remember, the core competencies need to be addressed in each of your responses.

Q21. Give me an example of a time when you have had to deal with a difficult student.

Sample Response

'As someone who has been teaching for the best part of 7 years now, I can safely say I've had more than my share of experience with misbehaving students!

One such occasion that I can remember was not too long ago. It was coming close to Christmas time, and students in my classes were becoming excited for the holidays. Inevitably, this meant that lessons were a little more rowdy, and the pupils were a bit harder to control. My Year 9 English group were due to sit an important examination right before they broke up for the holidays, and therefore it was essential for their lessons to run smoothly.

Unfortunately, there was one individual in the class who simply would not behave. Although I had previously taken him to one side to discuss his behaviour, he had not taken this on board, and continued to be rude and disrespectful to me during the lessons. The classroom learning assistant believed that I should send him to the headteacher, and punish him until he behaved himself. I did not believe that this would be the right thing to do. Although I wanted to take a hard line, I felt that it was important to identify why the pupil was acting this way rather than simply punishing him for it. The behaviour continued for 2 or 3 lessons before I decided to deal with it directly. I sought out the boy's form tutor, who told me that she had also had complaints from other staff members. Together we agreed that the right course of action would be to call the boy's parents into the school, and have a meeting with them.

After meeting with the student's parents, we discovered that there had recently been a death in their family. The boy was struggling to cope with the loss, and this was the reason he was 'acting out'. We arranged for the student in question to have regular visits to the school counsellor. The learning assistant and I also made sure to be extra vigilant in lessons to make sure the pupil was getting to grips with the material. As a result of all this, we witnessed a gradual improvement in behaviour, and the student ultimately achieved great marks in his end of term examination.

I believe that my actions really prevented a difficult situation from escalating. By not going straight to the headteacher, and determining to get to the bottom of the situation rather than just punishing the pupil, I initiated a course of action which saw an improvement in behaviour and grades. I took responsibility for the pupil and this had a positive impact.'

Q22. How would you deal with an exceptional student? Can you give me an example of when you've done this?

Sample Response

'I'm always delighted to have an exceptional student in my class, and there are several of these students who have stood out to me over the years.

During one of my first years at my previous school, I was teaching History to a Year 8 group. The class in question was completely new to me, and since it was September, they were tackling fresh material. One of the students, a young girl, was extremely active during the lessons and was constantly participating. I asked the class to submit a paper at the end of the month, and the student in question handed me back a piece of work which was so astoundingly brilliant, that I almost suspected her of cheating. The essay in question was at the very least Year 10-11 standard. After the next lesson, I called her back for a one-to-one chat to discuss the work. After reassuring her that she wasn't in trouble, I questioned her on the assignment and discovered that she was simply extremely interested in the subject and had conducted enormous amounts of research. As a teacher, there is nothing more refreshing to hear than a student willing and showing passion to learn, and I resolved to nurture this student's interest in the subject matter as much as I could over the next year.

With her form tutor and parent's permission, I lent the student in question a range of extra reading material, which I felt would really help to accelerate her learning. Of course, I made sure to extend the same courtesy to other members of the class too (although none of them took up the offer!) After a few months of continuously brilliant work from the student, I realised that it might be worth moving her onto a higher level. I sat down with my head of department and we agreed that it would be a good idea to put the student into a higher year group for her history lessons, on the grounds that she would be studying material more in line with her level. After discussing with her parents and ensuring the student was 100% happy with this, the student spent the rest of the year in a Year 10 History group. As the teacher of this class too, I was delighted to discover that she really applied herself and still turned in brilliant papers. Ultimately, the student went on to take the subject at A-level and the last I heard was that she was taking a doctorate in the subject.

As a teacher, nothing pleases me more than seeing my students engage in the subject and achieve success as a result.'

Q23. Tell me about the biggest challenge you have faced during your teaching career, and how you overcame this.

<u>Sample Response</u>

'I would say that my biggest challenge as a teacher has been in dealing with my own personal insecurities and doubts about myself.

When I started teaching, I was not exactly full of confidence. However, throughout my training and the past few years, I have slowly gained a belief that I am the right person to teach my students. At first I struggled with trusting in myself to deliver lessons, and was quite frankly terrified at the prospect of standing up in front of a class full of students. Although I had the subject knowledge and expertise, my mindset was not right.

After a month of theory-based PGCE, I quickly realised that I would have to take my own steps to fixing these issues, if I wanted to succeed as a teacher. Although the advice and help offered by my course was extremely helpful, I knew that this was an issue that came down to my strength of personality, and therefore something I would need to resolve on my own.

My first step was to start putting myself in situations where I would be utilising the skills required for teaching. Primarily, I wanted to ensure that I worked on my confidence and ability to speak in front of others. To this end, I joined a local 'speech givers' society in my town. The purpose of this group was to work on our speech giving abilities, learn top speaking tips and gain confidence. This society helped me to no end, and by the time my first placement came around, I was highly confident in my ability to lead a great lesson.

Along with a lack of confidence, I also realised that I had to start taking a firmer approach with my students. This was something that only became apparent when I actually started teaching. Although my students respected me, this lessened when it became apparent that I was reluctant to punish them for bad behaviour. I'm not a naturally angry or confrontational person, and enforcing discipline did not come easy for me. This caused a number of issues, so it was essential for me to resolve it. I sat down with my personal mentor and discussed my issues, and together we worked out a plan where I would gradually work my way into being stricter with students; starting by handing out smaller warnings/punishments, before moving up the scale. After some practice, I was able to implement these into my wider teaching, and the results were extremely positive.'

Q24. Can you give me an example of a time when you have had to deal with an angry parent?

<u>Sample Response</u>

'Yes, on many occasions actually. The most prominent incident that comes to mind was during my first job in a school. I had been working at the school for around 3 years at this point, and therefore was fairly experienced.

The class in question was a Year 9 Maths group. I had been having some behavioural problems with the class for a few lessons, in particular with one individual. The student in question wasn't paying attention, and was being highly disruptive. At the end of the previous lesson, I had set the group some homework to do to be handed in by the end of the week. Knowing full well that the student hadn't been paying attention, I called him behind after the lesson to make sure that he was okay to complete the homework and understood what was being asked. He confirmed to me that he did.

The afternoon after I had set the homework, I received a phone call in my office. The call was from the father of the boy who had been misbehaving in my lesson, and he was demanding a meeting. I agreed to sit down with him that evening, to discuss the issue. 2 hours later, the man arrived in my office. I could immediately tell that he was extremely angry, as he was speaking in a raised voice and waving his son's Maths homework book around in his hand. I calmly and professionally asked him to calm down, and take a seat. Although he continued waving the book around, he sat down and lowered the tone of his voice. I then asked the man to explain what the issue was and how he believed it could be resolved.

The man explained that his son had attempted to do the homework, but didn't have a clue how to do so. He believed this was evidence that his son hadn't been taught properly, and that it was unfair for me to set homework that students couldn't understand. His proposed resolution was that I set easier homework, and provide one-to-one tutoring for his son.

After the man had fully explained his issue, I clarified whether there was anything else he would like to add, before explaining my side of the story. I acknowledged that I was having difficulty teaching his son, but explained that this was because his son frequently misbehaved in lessons and did not pay attention. I also pointed out that I had directly asked his son about whether he understood the homework.

The man informed me that his son hadn't told him this, nor about the misbehaviour. I pointed out that I would be very happy to offer lunchtime support sessions to his son if required, although he would need to have a sit down with his son to discuss this.

My explanation immediately seemed to calm the man down, and he apologised for being so angry. He informed me that he'd had no idea his son was misbehaving. On my part, I acknowledged my error and that regardless of how the boy was acting in lessons; I should have done a better job in explaining the nature of the homework to him. Together we came to the conclusion that lunchtime learning sessions would be extremely useful, and the man went home to discuss this with his son. The next day, the boy came to me before the lesson and apologised, before agreeing to take part in a series of one-to-one revision sessions.

I believe that my calm and professional attitude, as well as my ability to take responsibility for my students, resolved a situation which could have got out of hand. Dealing with parents is an essential extension for teachers, as they are a huge part of our students' lives.'

Q25. Give me an example of a time when you have utilised your organisational skills.

Sample Response

'As an experienced teacher, I don't think a day goes by without me having to utilise my organisational skills! This is particularly the case during exam time, as I can recall with a previous class of mine.

The class in question was a Year 9 English group, who had big examinations coming up. Whilst I was not their regular teacher, I was required to step in and take over their lessons in the run up to their exam, as their teacher was off sick. After just one lesson, it became apparent to me that the class were woefully underprepared for their examination. Their textual analysis skills (which were essential for the test) were extremely poor and they had no concept of what they would be asked to do during the examination. Having been given a timetable for teaching by the absent teacher, I quickly realised that this wouldn't be sufficient, and that we wouldn't have nearly enough time to incorporate her plans. Therefore, I had to take the initiative, and devise my own timetable for this class.

In order to do this, the first thing I needed to assess was how strong the class were in essential areas. Since we had only a month before the exam, with 4 lessons per week; it was important to make a decision on which topics would be given the most attention. After a disastrous first lesson, where it became apparent that the class were miles behind, I set about creating a test for the second lesson. This would allow me to assess the general knowledge of the group. As expected, the results came back fairly weak; but they did provide me with a learning pattern. I used these results to form a learning timetable over the weekend.

On Monday, first lesson, I spent the first 10 minutes providing the class with a detailed calendar of what topics we would be tackling and also links for key reading material. I felt this was very important to do. Not only was I showing them respect and treating them like adults, but if they could prepare and read material in advance of the classes, then the lessons would be much more focused and efficient as a result.

Following this, we got started. Although not all of the class took to the lessons, which were admittedly very intense, the vast majority of the group were fully behind the task and understood the importance. When the class got their results back, almost every single member of the group achieved at least a grade B.

While I was disappointed that not every member of the class had achieved a B or higher, I was proud of myself for organising the lessons in such an efficient manner; with such little notice or preparation time. I did my utmost to ensure that the class caught up on the material to a level where they could achieve good results, and to make sure that they understood the seriousness of the next month of lessons. When the teacher in question returned, I had a serious sit down with her to inform her about the situation and how poorly prepared her class were. She acknowledged that she had been teaching badly due to her illness, and resolved not to put her students' learning at risk in the future.'

Q26. Can you give me an example of a time when you have demonstrated your flexibility?

<u>Sample Response</u>

'I'm a highly flexible person, and have demonstrated this on a number of occasions throughout my teacher training.

The best example of this was during my first teaching placement in a school. As I'm sure you can imagine, this was an extremely nerve-wracking experience, and there were so many things that needed to be organised beforehand. Even though you have conducted extensive observation and theory lessons prior to the experience, there's nothing that can really prepare you for the real thing!

Unfortunately, my first lesson as a trainee teacher – actually teaching – was anything but smooth! I had prepared a full lesson plan, but this quickly began to fall apart as the lesson progressed. First, one of the students in my class had a severe nosebleed, and had to be sent to the medical room. This caused a huge scene in the lesson and distracted the class for over 10 minutes. Secondly, the class in question became aware of how nervous I was, and smelled blood (no pun intended!) Their behaviour was poor throughout the lesson, and I came away from the lesson feeling really upset.

After sitting down with my mentor, she explained to me that I simply hadn't been flexible enough with my lesson plan, and that it was important not to let the experience negatively affect me. She persuaded me to go into the next lesson with a more open approach. She discussed how I might need to deviate from my plan in order to accommodate the changing nature of a lesson.

So, I took this advice on board for my second lesson, and took a far more flexible approach. When the class started misbehaving, I thought about the reasons why they were misbehaving rather than simply trying to force my lesson on them, and altered my approach. I didn't panic, and the class was far more organised as a result. I took this advice on board throughout my time in PGCE teaching placements. Although I understand that it is not always the right thing to allow a class's behaviour to dictate the lesson, I believe it's extremely important to be flexible and understand that adjustments sometimes need to be made; particularly in such a combustible and changeable environment.'

Q27. Here at Ficshire Academy, we really value teamwork amongst our staff. Tell me about a time when you have demonstrated your teamwork abilities.

<u>Sample Response</u>

'As someone who has worked in teams on an almost constant basis, I can say unequivocally that I have great teamwork skills. Although I appreciate the value of working solo, and understand that teaching involves working alone a lot of the time; there really is no substitute for working in a team in my opinion.

Proof of this can be found when looking at what I achieved in my last position. Along with teaching, I was given the role of coordinating with parents from the students in Years 8 and 9. This meant that I was responsible for creating learning initiatives, ensuring students were behaving themselves, and writing up progress reports.

This was a big job, and not something that could be conducted by me alone. In order to succeed in the role, I needed to coordinate and communicate with a wide range of other staff members at the school. This meant having one-to-one meetings with these staff members if necessary. For example, if a particular student in a particular class was struggling with History, I'd have a sit down with that teacher to discuss why they were struggling and how this could be improved. If disciplinary measures were needed, I was also responsible for meeting with parents to discuss the situation.

Throughout all of these meetings, I needed to work with the individuals in question, to produce a positive solution. This meant utilising all of the fundamental qualities required for teamwork: good communication, professionalism, integrity and honesty.

I made sure in every single instance that the students in question and the individuals whom I was working with, were 100% satisfied with the agreed resolutions, and that clear steps were agreed in order to carry this out.'

Q28. Give me an example of a time when you have worked successfully with a teaching assistant.

<u>Sample Response</u>

'I have worked with many different teaching assistants in my classrooms, all at varying levels of expertise.

During my last position, I was required to work with a teaching assistant who was fairly new to the role. She had just finished her training and was conducting a period of assistance in the classroom, before she would aim to go on and become a teacher herself. As someone with many years of experience, I resolved to take her under my wing and help her become a great teacher.

On the first day that the assistant entered my classroom, she was extremely nervous, and actually seemed scared of the students. I noticed this straight away, took her to one side and assured her that I had complete confidence in her ability; and that she could come to me if she needed any help. I explained what I would require her to do during the lesson and gave her some brief pointers on how to go about doing these. I made sure to confirm that she was 100% happy and clear with this before we started teaching.

As the lesson progressed, I went round the room working with different groups of students. I asked the teaching assistant to do the same, and at some points we met in the middle and conducted in-depth discussion with the students together. I was really impressed by the depth of her knowledge, but did notice one or two pointers which I could give feedback on. At all times, I made sure to encourage the assistant and engage with her on a subject level. I felt it was important to increase her confidence and show her that she was truly capable of being a great teacher.

At the end of the lesson, I sat down with the assistant to give her some feedback. I made sure that I provided her with lots of praise for the level of subject knowledge she had displayed and the way she had integrated herself with the class, despite being nervous beforehand. I gave her some pointers on communication and getting her ideas across to the students. Overall, I made sure that she felt good about her own performance and happy that she was on the right track.

I am pleased to say that after a few months of working together, the assistant went on to complete her integration into teaching and became a fantastic teacher, in a nearby school.'

Q29. Give me an example of when you have taken direct action to improve a student's performance.

<u>Sample Response</u>

'It's always disappointing to me when a student is underperforming, but I am someone who will always go above and beyond to make sure all of my students are up to (and beyond) the required level.

A good example of this was in my final placement during my PGCE training. By this point, I was leading classes myself and had full responsibility for teaching the students. Unfortunately, I had one student in my Year 10 History class, who was really struggling. This was even more surprising to me, as the student in question had achieved exceptional grades in his mid-year examination and was generally considered one of the brightest students in the year. Since I had taken over the History lessons, his grades had plummeted, and he did not seem to be making any effort to engage with the subject. Although I repeatedly tried my best with the student, and made every attempt to involve him, he refused to engage and his performance in lessons got worse and worse. This was even more confusing to me, as the rest of the class were getting on great with the subject material and I hadn't had any problems with them.

After attempting to tackle the problem head on, by speaking to the student directly (which didn't work as he didn't respond to me) I decided to speak to one of his friends. While I did consider his form tutor as an option, I was aware that the student's grades hadn't suffered in any other subject, and wondered whether his performance in History was purely down to his reaction to a new teacher taking over. My suspicions were confirmed when his friend informed me that the student had a very close relationship with his previous teacher (who I had taken over from) and was very upset to have received someone new.

In order to resolve this, the first thing I did was meet with the previous teacher, who agreed to meet with the student to try and reassure him that he was in capable hands. After this meeting took place, and before our next lesson, I took the student to one side and assured him that I wanted us to get along and to provide him with the best learning experience possible. I asked him to try his best and that I was always available if he needed extra help. To my relief, the student was far more involved in the lesson, and after the lesson, actually approached me to apologise for his behaviour. From that point forward, I had no issues with the pupil, and his performance improved substantially as a result.'

Q30. Do you have any experience of dealing with drugs or alcohol on school grounds? What did you do? If not, how would you deal with this situation?

<u>Sample Response</u>

'Thankfully, my experience of dealing with these issues is limited at best. However there was one incident that I can remember, involving alcohol.

The incident occurred during my second year of working at my first school. I was on my way out of school at the end of the day, when I witnessed three Year 9 students huddled behind the bike sheds inside the school gates. The students appeared to be drinking from a bottle of vodka, and were behaving erratically. I immediately approached the students and questioned them on the contents of the bottle. When they denied that the contents were alcoholic, I confiscated the bottle from them. I could immediately smell that they were indeed drinking vodka, and to my alarm the students appeared to be drunk.

My first course of action was to take them to the medical room. I informed the medical staff about the situation and also provided them with the bottle from which the students had been drinking. With permission from the nurse, I then went to speak directly to the student services department, which immediately made contact with the headmaster.

I was then asked to give a statement about the incident and exactly what occurred. The students in question were suspended. The important thing about this issue was the wellbeing of the students. Crucially, they were not substantially harmed.

I believe that my actions were extremely important in this instance. Alcohol is absolutely unacceptable on school premises, and I made sure that I followed the school's policy on this down to a tee. Due to my actions, the students in question were unharmed, and learned a valuable lesson.'

Q31. What is your personal policy on bullying, and how have you demonstrated this in the past?

<u>Sample Response</u>

'My personal policy on bullying is of absolutely no-tolerance, and I would fully expect any school that I am working at to take the same attitude. School should be a place where students feel safe, and it is essential for schools and the teachers working within them, to foster a caring and welfare-orientated environment.

Whilst working at my previous school, I had to deal with at least one bullying incident. One of these incidents occurred between three of the students in my form group. The bullying first came to my attention when I witnessed one of the students crying outside of the classroom. After comforting and questioning the individual, who wouldn't tell me what the problem was, I resolved to keep a close eye on the situation in the future. I didn't have to wait long, as the very next day I witnessed a scene outside of the school gates where two students from my form group appeared to be teasing and picking on the aforementioned pupil, who seemed very upset. I witnessed this again during form time, and decided to take action. I asked the student who was upset to stay behind at the end, and quizzed him on the nature of the interaction. He confessed that the other two pupils had been teasing him for a long time now, and at times had become physically aggressive with him. He had asked them to stop, but they had refused, and he had started to dread coming to school.

Realising that I was dealing with a bullying incident, I immediately took a statement from the student and asked him if he would be happy to come with me to student services. I assured him that he wasn't in any trouble, and that I would do everything possible to resolve the situation for him and prevent this from happening again. I made sure I comforted the student and made it clear that this kind of behaviour would not be tolerated. Once we arrived at student services, I sat with the student as they took a statement from him. We then interviewed the two pupils who had been bullying him, who at first denied culpability, but soon admitted to their behaviour. Together with student services, we firmly demonstrated to the two students that their behaviour was wrong and their parents were called. The two boys were suspended.

Student services thanked me for my actions, and asked me to keep a close eye on the student who had been the victim of such unacceptable behaviour. I feel that my observation and resultant action played a key role in resolving this situation, and ensuring that the pupil in question could come to school unafraid and feel respected by those within the school. Bullying of any kind should not be tolerated.'

Q32. How do you define bullying? Is there any grey area on this matter for you, and if so, give me an example.

Sample Response

'As I mentioned, I consider bullying in any form to be completely unacceptable, and would expect any school to take the same attitude. However, I do understand that not everyone can get along at all times during school hours. Schoolchildren are at an age where there will inevitably be squabbles and arguments, and sometimes this can get out of hand. As teachers, we should do our best to promote a harmonious and peaceful environment. No student should have to come to school fearing for their safety or wellbeing, and we should take direct action to prevent this from happening.

A good example of this would be when I was working in my first placement on the PGCE. One of my students came to me during form time, highly distressed and upset. After I enquired about the situation, he explained to me that a fellow student had asked him, 'Do you go to English club?' The student had taken this extremely offensively. He believed that the student was mocking him to his face, and informed me that he had been 'bullied'. After seeking clarification on the latter, I was informed that this accusation was based solely on this incident, and not on any other. He believed that he had been targeted because of his ginger hair. I did my best to comfort the student, and then sought out the student who had asked him the question.

The student who had been accused seemed extremely surprised by this, and immediately apologised for any offence that had been caused. He explained that he had simply wanted to know what time the club was running after school, and that he hadn't mocked or bullied the student. I asked the two students to shake hands, before resolving to keep a close eye on the situation in the future. Thus, a difficult situation was defused, and no further action needed to be taken. This was simply a mix-up, and certainly did not constitute bullying.'

Q33. Let's say you are teaching a lesson. All of a sudden, a student throws a rubber across the room. It hits you in the head. What do you do?

Sample Response

'I would take immediate action. Not only would this constitute an act of severe disrespect, but it also presents a major health and safety issue. Both myself and fellow pupils are in danger of being injured by behaviour such as this, and therefore it would be essential for me to take a no-tolerance approach.

First of all, I'd speak to the student and make it clear that this was completely unacceptable. I would clearly show why this is unacceptable and that it breaches the school's disciplinary policy, before moving them either out of the class or to another side of the room – on their own and away from the other students. If necessary, I might send them to a senior member of staff.

Finally, I would issue a disciplinary order (such as a detention) and inform them that future poor behaviour would lead to more severe/ escalating punishment. I may also call them behind after the lesson to discuss the incident further.

While no teacher likes to discipline their students, I fully understand that this is completely necessary from time to time and we must ensure that our students have a healthy level of respect for the rules of the school.'

Q34. How important do you consider the layout of a classroom to be, and is there any particular way in which you would lay your classroom out?

<u>Sample Response</u>

'As someone who is highly organised, I'm a firm believer in the importance of classroom layout and seating plans!

When organising the layout of my classroom, I always take the following factors into consideration:

-Firstly, I make sure that every single member of the class can see me, and that I can see them. As a teacher, it's obviously essential that you can monitor the behaviour of the class, but in the same way, the class will quickly become disinterested or distracted if they can't see you or the board. This is what leads to problems such as misbehaviour, as those students don't feel included in the lesson.

-Secondly, I place students in a position where they can interact with each other. Group work is a big factor in my lessons. I am a teacher who preaches active learning, rather than passive, and therefore I want my students to get involved and share ideas.

-Thirdly, ease of access. Since I use lots of group work, I spend time going round each group. Therefore, it's important for me to have a clear space in which I can operate and move around freely.

-Finally, I think it is important that a classroom is laid out to minimise risk of any safety issues. There needs to be space for students to be able to safely move around the classroom. Each student needs to feel comfortable, and not feel squashed or isolated.

Since I'm a big believer in 'visual value', I like to make sure the room is colourful, any aesthetic learning materials are clear and bold, and that every element of the room serves some purpose in aiding the flow of a positive lesson.'

Q35. Give me an example of a time when you have had to work under pressure.

<u>Sample Response</u>

'Throughout my PGCE course, I have been under constant pressure with deadlines. Combined with lesson planning, placements and teaching, this made for perhaps one of the most difficult but rewarding years of my life.

I would say that the climax of this came during late April, when I had two course-changing assignments due in, whilst at the same time was teaching 4 days a week in placement schools. This was incredibly stressful, but I'm extremely proud of how I managed my time and work under such pressurised circumstances.

Knowing how difficult the month would be, I sat down at the start of the month and planned out exactly how and when I would go about taking key tasks, managing my essays and planning/teaching lessons at the same time. While I understood that school placements would take up the majority of my time, I was absolutely determined to achieve top marks in my assessments. At the same time however, I acknowledged that my performance in both areas would suffer if I did not make time for myself – so it was important to find the right balance.

With careful planning and organisation, creating a detailed timetable that listed when and where each task would be carried out (and sticking to it!) I managed to balance out the month and received top marks in my essays, all the while teaching great lessons in my placement schools.

The biggest thing I have learned from this experience is that you can't always plan to perfection, especially with teaching. A teacher's day doesn't end when the school day finishes, and there are always unexpected issues that can come up. Luckily, I am prepared to take on any challenge, regardless of how unexpected it is. I'm entirely flexible, too.'

Q36. In this school, we really encourage our students to be creative and think outside of the box. How do you approach creativity in the classroom? Give me an example of when you have tapped into the creative side of your students.

Sample Response

'I'm aware of the fact that your school is so encouraging of creativity, and this is actually one of the reasons that I would love to teach here.

I'm a very creative person myself, being an English student who is currently in the process of writing her own novel, and therefore I would absolutely welcome creativity with open arms. I know that some teachers in this country are scrutinised for 'robotic' approaches to teaching, and I really want to be a part of improving students' creative and individual mindsets. As teachers, we should do everything that we can to encourage our students to think 'outside of the box' whilst still recognising that solutions can also be found 'inside the box', so to speak.

Throughout my training, I have done my utmost to get my students thinking creatively and in an original way about the subject. I actually feel that my own writing experience comes in really useful here, especially when analysing texts. One way that I like to introduce students to a new book is to ask them to draw character plotlines and write down their thoughts on the book. So, for example, if we've just started a book and been introduced to a specific character, I like to ask the class to write down their impressions of the character and what they think their motivations will be. We then compare this against the way the character is written. I've always found that this creates great discussion and really gets the group thinking about why things are written in the way that they are. Another exercise that I like to do is to ask the class to write a paragraph from a character in the book's perspective. This gets them thinking outside of their own head, about other motivations, and the way that other's think. I think this is great for stimulating the mind and encouraging creativity.

Overall, creativity is really important and I believe that it's one of the most important qualities for us to foster.'

Q37. Picture the scenario. A parent has written a note excusing their child for not completing their homework, because they had football training. What do you do?

Sample Response

'I would take a calm and reasonable approach to this scenario, whilst standing firm on the fact that homework and schoolwork should come before the student's football training. My reaction would largely depend on whether this was a one-off occurrence. If it was, then I would take steps to ensure that it didn't happen again. I would first relay my concerns to the child, before contacting his parent to clarify the situation and ensure that this was resolved as amicably as possible. I would make sure that the parent understood the seriousness of my concern and that school policy was being followed. I would also endeavour to make sure that the homework was actually completed, and not just skipped altogether. If I set homework, then there is a reason for this: it will have an educational benefit for the child. It is imperative that they don't miss out.

If this was a repeat offence, then I would take more serious action. Not only would I get in touch with the parents to try and organise a meeting, but I would also contact the head of year and the student's form tutor. By involving other individuals who are in a position to assist with this, we can work as a team to resolve the situation.

At all times, I make sure I follow school policy. Schoolwork comes first.'

Q38. Tell me about the most difficult student that you have ever worked with. How did you deal with this?

Sample Response

'After 2 years teaching in my first job, I was assigned a Year 10 class. The school was mixed, so the class had both boys and girls. In this class, I encountered not 1 but 2 of the most challenging pupils I have ever faced. The two pupils were named Henry and Katie.

From the very first lesson, Henry and Katie caused me no end of problems. Katie was extremely rude and talked loudly over the top of my instructions to the class. Henry had a habit of tossing random objects across the room. Even after I sent him to the headmaster's office for throwing a compass, his behaviour did not stop. Katie wasn't just rude to me, but to her classmates, too. After speaking to some of the pupils after my lessons, they informed me that they had felt personally victimised by her behaviour. While I didn't feel like this was an incident of bullying, I was extremely concerned by the impact that Katie's aggressive behaviour was having on other students. While Henry was not being nasty to other students, his behaviour continued to escalate and eventually I had him removed from my classes altogether, learning in a separate room. However, this didn't mean I had given up. I strongly felt that Henry in particular just needed guidance. He was a frequent underperformer in examinations, and had personally admitted to me that he felt 'too stupid' for the school.

The first thing I did was to contact the school counsellor. I felt that Henry would be much better off having someone to talk to, who could encourage him and build his confidence up. I believed his misbehaviour was a result of a lack of confidence, which manifested itself in disruptive actions. I also offered lunchtime-learning sessions to Henry, so that he could catch up on the material. These sessions gave me a great chance to get to know Henry on a one-to-one basis, engage with him and discourage his bad behaviour. I persuaded Henry that if he could behave, he would be allowed back into my class. After meeting with both his form tutor and his parents, we agreed to make a sustained effort to get Henry back into the classroom and behaving himself again. Unfortunately, in his first lesson back in my classroom, Henry hit another student over the head with a Geography book. As a result, he was suspended indefinitely. While I was absolutely devastated by this, I was also confident in the knowledge that I had done my utmost to resolve the situation and tried to amend his bad behaviour.

At the same time, I was also trying to resolve the situation with Katie.

It emerged that Katie was having a number of problems at home. Her behaviour seemed to have rapidly declined since these problems started; previously she was achieving top-level marks in all of her subjects.

The first thing that concerned me was Katie's behaviour towards other students. While I wanted to help her, it was imperative to me that other students weren't being negatively impacted by her actions. I spoke to the pupils who had been affected and clarified that they didn't feel they had been bullied. They confirmed this, but they were worried that Katie might start to become physically aggressive. I recognised that this was far more than just a 'subject problem'. By this I mean that the problem was not confined just to my lessons, so it was extremely important for me to involve other professionals in the issue, including her form tutor and her parents. Unfortunately, Katie's parents proved extremely uncooperative. When myself and her form tutor sat down with them to discuss the issue, they simply laughed at us and we were informed that 'school is for suckers'. This was extremely worrying. My colleague suggested that we get in touch with social services about this issue. While I felt this was the right course of action, I also wanted to seek clarification from other authorities in the school – namely the headmaster and head of year. I arranged a meeting between all of the involved members of staff, to discuss the scenario. We felt that it would be beneficial to wait before taking such drastic action, and see if we could amend Katie's performance in school ourselves. If this didn't work, we'd have to get other professionals involved.

I was given the task of monitoring Katie's subject performance in my lessons. Although I had taken a leading role in dealing with the issue, and wanted to help as much as I could, I recognised that there is a time and a place for this and that there were others who were more suited for dealing with Katie's personal issues than myself. For my part, I tried my very best to improve Katie's performance and through much hard work managed to get her grade up from a D to a B. At all times I made her feel supported and appreciated, whilst still being absolutely firm on the consequences of further bad behaviour.

The end result of this was that Katie's performance in my subject improved, and so did her confidence. She became friendlier towards her classmates. We did not have to call social services in the end, as her situation at home was resolved. Although we were extremely lucky, I believe we made the right choice by choosing to deal with the issue internally and preventing things from escalating. I feel that my part in this was extremely important, as I recognised the problem and played a key part in the solution.'

Q39. Tell me about a time when you have dealt with a volatile incident in the classroom.

Sample Response

'Whilst teaching in an all-girl school, I had to deal with an incident between two pupils in my Year 11 Maths group. The two girls, Katie and Gemma, had previously been best friends. It had come to my attention that they were now sitting on other sides of the classroom. While I had noticed this, it hadn't caused any issues so far. Disagreements are part of school life and I expected them to make up sooner or later.

Unfortunately, as soon as I entered the classroom, it became apparent to me that the atmosphere was fairly hostile. The two girls were trading nasty comments across the room. I asked them to keep things down, so that I could teach the lesson. Although they did this for a few minutes, things immediately picked up again soon after, and then things took a turn for the worse.

Gemma got up out of her seat, walked over to Katie and struck her across the face. Katie responded by scratching her, and then the two started scrapping on the desk. I immediately rushed over to try and separate the girls, who at this point were screaming and becoming increasingly violent. I pulled Katie away from Gemma, who had a bloody nose. I immediately asked a responsible member of the class to take Gemma to the medical office, and explain to the office staff what had happened. They would then alert the senior management. I checked that Katie hadn't been significantly harmed by the exchange, and then asked another member of the class to supervise the group, whilst I escorted her to the office of the head of year.

After explaining the situation to the head of year, I then went back to my class and finished the rest of the lesson, before contacting the head of year later to explain the end result of the scenario.

I feel that my actions were important in resolving the situation. Not only did I make sure the girls were separated immediately, but I also did not allow the rest of the class to be significantly impacted by the disruption. I understood that there were professionals better placed to deal with the scenario than me. What I did learn from the scenario was that tension in the classroom should not be ignored, as this can swiftly escalate. I should have acknowledged or tried to resolve the issue earlier, and this was my mistake. I have learned from this and applied this lesson to similar scenarios since.'

Q40. Give me an example of a time when you have used criticism constructively.

Sample Response

'I am someone who is able to take criticism extremely well, and always do my best to handle it in as constructive a manner as possible. I believe this is something that originally resulted from my university degree, where I was subjected to large amounts of criticism and honest feedback. As a result, I have developed thick skin, and am now able to use constructive feedback to my advantage.

A good example of this was during my previous position as a History teacher. One of my lessons was observed by my head of department. This was a yearly observation, which was conducted during regular lesson time, with the aim of assessing the continuous quality of members of staff at the school.

Although I felt that the lesson went really well, my head of department had a few things to give feedback on, that she felt I could improve. I was surprised by this, but I took her feedback with an open mind and fully accepted the comments.

Her primary concern was that I was perhaps pushing the students in my class a little too hard. As she correctly pointed out, we were not due to cover the area of the curriculum that I had been teaching for another week. Feeling that my class were up to the challenge, I had pushed ahead early for this. I agreed with her that I had overestimated the group, who were not quite ready for the new material. I have a tendency to be a little too enthusiastic with pushing the learning boundaries of my pupils. While this can pay off, and there are good intentions behind it, I accept that there is a time and a place for this.

Using the feedback provided, I made immediate changes to my next lesson, which had involved trying to incorporate the same approach. I was flexible enough to recognise that I had made a mistake and learned from the feedback from my head of department.

Although I am a highly experienced professional, who has taught for a great number of years, I am still capable of improvement and absolutely welcome the opportunity to do so.'

Q41. Thinking back on your own experiences of attending school, how do you think this has shaped you as a teacher?

Sample Response

'I believe that my experience of school has had a huge bearing on the way I am as a teacher. My experience of school was largely a mixed bag of negative and positive experiences.

On the one hand, I believe that attending school had a significant impact on the way I viewed teachers. While I was at school, teachers were inspirational figures for me, who provided care and support and nurtured me throughout my childhood. As you spend the majority of your childhood in a school, it's essential that figures like these are present to offer wisdom and guidance. As teachers, we are a daily source of support for students. We are given huge responsibility and placed in a hugely privileged position; entrusted by parents with their children. It is our duty to give back and earn their trust. I can safely say that the teachers in my school inspired me hugely when considering this career.

On the other hand, it's fair to say that I didn't have the most positive experience with other pupils at my school. From my experience, children were very unkind and at times I felt unfairly victimised. While teachers can provide support; school is very difficult if the other pupils aren't being pleasant towards you. This is one of the reasons why I want to teach though. Teaching isn't just about the subject matter; it's about helping students to become responsible and caring adults. As a teacher, you play a leading role in ensuring that school is a caring and enjoyable place to be. Although the teachers at my school were fantastic in an individual sense, they did not foster this attitude, and I suffered as a result. I want to be different, and to establish a caring and responsible atmosphere at the school where I work.'

Q42. Give me an example of a time when you have worked constructively, to resolve an issue with a work colleague.

Sample Response

'Very recently, when I was working in my current role, I had an issue with a teacher from another department.

Every Tuesday morning, my Year 9 English group would arrive at least 10 minutes late for their lesson. After questioning the group on why they were always late, I was informed that their Maths teacher was keeping them behind every lesson; for misbehaviour and other reasons. This was extremely frustrating for me, and it cut out an important section of my lesson plan.

My first step was to try and encourage the class to behave in their Maths lesson. I fully understood that their teacher might have been frustrated, and I didn't want to exasperate this issue by asking him to change the way he ran his lessons. Unfortunately, this didn't work. Upon further questioning, the class admitted that they didn't feel they had misbehaved and were unsure as to why the teacher was keeping them behind.

I decided to tackle the problem head on. Without needing to be confrontational, I sent the teacher in question a polite email explaining the problem and asking him to try and get in touch to resolve it. The teacher in question responded back almost immediately, questioning the accuracy of my claims. I asked him to take a look at his 'sign out-logbook' which we used to show when a lesson was finished, to show that I was right. He then apologised wholeheartedly and informed me that he hadn't realised his lessons had been overrunning, and would do his utmost to send his class out on time in the future. This fixed the problem, and my class were on time for the rest of their lessons.

I believe I acted professionally, responsibly, and with the right amount of restraint in dealing with this situation. I was polite at all times, and respected the needs of my fellow teacher in dealing with his classroom situation. We resolved things constructively, and this was to the benefit of everyone.'

Q43. It's revision time at school, and students have exams coming up. How do you help your students to prepare?

Sample Response

'Luckily I'm very experienced with this topic! As I explained earlier, I'm very big on interactive learning; and this means that revision sessions in my lessons are always a lot of fun for students.

I fully understand that revision isn't necessarily something that students want to be doing, but it is a necessary evil. This is the reason why I try to make my revision sessions as engaging and interesting as possible. In the past, I have made the mistake of taking a more 'generic' approach to revision lessons, and the results have almost never been positive. At the same time though, I do understand that the central aim of revision should be to consolidate learning, and therefore fun should never come at the expense of knowledge. If the students aren't learning, then it's just a waste of time. It's also important to pick age-appropriate revision exercises, depending on the group you are teaching.

As a language teacher, one of my favourite revision exercises is to play a game of language Pictionary. One person or group describes/draws an item or word, and then the rest of the class have to put the word in a sentence or just guess it. I have found that this really stimulates students and gets them to remember things and associate them with specific elements. I also like to use PowerPoints, and incorporate video clips and interactive materials into my slides.

Overall, I'd say I take a very proactive approach to revision, which reflects upon my style as a teacher.'

Q44. Our school contains an extremely diverse community of pupils. As a teacher, how do you teach your students to accept other cultures?

Sample Response

'Respect for diversity is extremely important to me. As a teacher and an individual, I am always tolerant and understanding of other cultures and I think it's a fantastic thing that schools in the UK contain such a variety of races and cultures. Students who can learn to work collaboratively with classmates from different backgrounds will be far better prepared for the world around them. Ignorance breeds hate, and therefore learning acceptance, tolerance and kindness is the best way forward.

When teaching my lessons, I always make sure that:

A – Every single student feels respected and that the class as a whole demonstrates an acceptance of diversity. This is absolutely essential.

B – Every single student has their cultural needs met and that my teaching style does not infringe upon or isolate any member of the class. Teaching is universal, it is not a case of 'the needs of the many' nor is it fair to focus all of my attention on one particular pupil. I make sure that every pupil is happy.

As an English teacher, I use different cultures as a constant reference point. It's important to get students thinking about the way that others experience the world, and why their values are just as important. Comparing and contrasting cultures, and showing students the overwhelming value of other belief systems and opinions; is extremely important.'

Q45. Give me an example of when you have demonstrated a respect for diversity as a teacher.

Sample Response

'As someone currently teaching at a hugely diverse school, I am extremely comfortable and familiar with teaching students from different cultures or backgrounds, and making sure that their needs are met. I have a great knowledge of religions such as Hinduism, Islam and Christianity; and likewise of countries which might not be as prominent here in the UK. This means that I am in a fantastic position to provide my students with understanding and acceptance.

A good example of this was very recently, during Ramadan. I had a Muslim student in my class who was fasting. The student in question was very young. As per the requirements of Ramadan, the student could not eat or drink between daylight hours. As it happened, this particular period of Ramadan coincided with some extremely hot weather.

As a result, I noticed that the student in question was showing signs of dehydration during the lesson. He seemed extremely tired, was sweating profusely and had informed me that he felt ill. I was immediately concerned for the wellbeing of the student. I sat down next to him and asked him whether he would be okay to take a glass of water. When he informed me that he could not, as it would break his fast, I gently persuaded him that in this situation, it would be acceptable for him to do so. I informed him that Islamic teaching allows for Muslims to break their fast in the circumstance that they become ill, and make it up later. I demonstrated an understanding and acceptance of his faith and assured him that it was okay for him to take a glass of water. He agreed with me, and I then sent him down to the sick room for a further check-up.

I felt I acted responsibly in this situation, whilst still ensuring that I maintained a good level of respect for the student's faith. Because of my knowledge and understanding of other cultures and beliefs, I was able to persuade the student to take the safe and risk-free option, in a manner that did not offend him and kept to school policy.'

Q46. Give me an example of a time when you have dealt with a distressed student, who wasn't in your class.

Sample Response

'When I was working in my previous position, I encountered a difficult situation.

I was one of the last teachers to leave the school at the end of the day. As I walked out of the gates, I saw a young student standing by the entrance to the school, looking distressed. Upon asking them whether they were okay, the student informed me that her parents had forgotten to pick her up, and that she had no way to contact them.

My first priority was to comfort the student and inform her that she didn't need to worry, as we would resolve the situation for her. I assured her we would do everything possible to contact her parents and get her home okay. I took her inside the reception area of the school, sat her down and asked her several questions, including:

'What time were your parents meant to pick you up?'

'Can you think of any reason why they might have been delayed?'

'Do you have a number to contact them on?'

When the student informed me that her parents were meant to collect her 2 hours earlier, and that she didn't have a number, I used the school directory to obtain a contact number. Unfortunately, nobody was picking up! The school secretary informed me that she would be at the premises for a few hours more, so she suggested that it might be a good idea for me to try and drive the student to her house and see if anybody was in. I felt that this was a good idea, but also wanted to sign some paperwork first to clarify that it was okay for me to do this. I was aware that the student's parents might have been unhappy for me to take her off the premises without permission.

After signing some paperwork, I drove the student to her home and came out with her while she knocked on the door. Luckily her Mother was there to answer. She was relieved to see her child and thanked me so much for bringing her home. She informed me that because there was a power cut in their street, she had no way of contacting the school, and because she couldn't drive, she had no way to come and pick the girl up. Her husband, who was meant to be picking her up, was stuck in London! She apologised sincerely for the trouble.

I thanked her for explaining and assured her that it was no trouble.

However, I was concerned that the parent in question had apparently failed to go out of her way to resolve the situation for herself. While I didn't mention this to her, I did bring it up to a member of the student services team at school, who assured me that they would look into the matter.

I feel that my actions were highly responsible, and saved the student a great deal of distress. As a teacher, you aren't just in charge with looking after the students in your classes, but all of the students at the school.'

Q47. Give me an example of a time when you have dealt with an adult situation in the classroom (i.e. teenage pregnancy).

Sample Response

'I can remember one particularly serious situation, from a few years ago…

I had just finished teaching my final lesson of the day, a Year 11 Geography class. As I was packing my things away, a girl from the class approached my desk. She seemed to be extremely tearful and upset. She asked me if she could tell me about a personal issue in confidence.

I assured her that I was there to support her and that I was more than happy for her to share her issue in confidence with me, but I also made it clear that I couldn't maintain this confidence if the issue risked her personal safety or that of others, or if she had knowledge of a crime. She then confessed to me that she was pregnant, but didn't know who the father was, and that she hadn't told anyone else about it.

My first reaction to this was to assure her that I wouldn't tell anyone else about this, and that her secret was safe with me. However, I then took steps to encourage her to speak to others about the issue, especially her parents. I asked her whether she had been to see a doctor (which she hadn't), and whether she knew much about pregnancy. She didn't, so I decided to take a few steps to help her.

I logged onto my computer and found a few pieces of really useful advice on the NHS website. I then printed these out for her, along with a PDF leaflet. I encouraged her to read through all of the material, and assured her that I would always be here to talk about the issue/ to offer support. At all times I made sure that she felt comforted and supported and knew that I would keep her confidence. I demonstrated my listening and communication skills throughout, to help her feel safe.

I feel that I took a highly professional and responsible approach to this situation. With my support, the student was now prepared to make an informed decision on what to do with her baby.'

Q48. Can you give me an example of a time when you have dealt with an unprofessional colleague in school?

<u>Sample Response</u>

'When I was working at my previous school, I encountered a serious situation with a close colleague of mine.

The individual in question had been going through a rough time in his personal life. He had recently split with his wife and was not dealing with this particularly well. While both myself and other staff at the school had advised him to take time off to deal with this, he had refused to do this and continued to come in regardless.

On the day in question, I had just arrived at the school when my colleague approached me. I immediately noticed that he was slurring his speech badly, and seemed uncoordinated. He was drunk. I was appalled by this situation, and asked him what he was doing in school in such a state. When he could not give me a coherent answer, I immediately decided to take action.

First of all I informed him that he was not fit to teach on this day. There was no way he was in a state to teach a class, nor could he remain on the premises. I decided to take him straight to the head teacher's office. Although I did not want to get my colleague into trouble, I felt that this was the only solution. Cover needed to be arranged for his lessons, and arrangements needed to be made to escort him off the premises. As I was teaching classes within the next half hour, I was not available to take him home and it would have been wrong to disrupt the timetable of my student's/teaching to do this. It was also imperative that the head teacher understood the gravity of the situation.

I brought my colleague to the headmistress, who was extremely worried about him, and immediately arranged for someone to take him home. She thanked me for doing the responsible thing and promised me that she would work to resolve the situation. My colleague was sent home and although he received a suspension, he then took time off and came back much better for it. I felt that my actions were essential in making this happen.'

Q49. Give me an example of a time when you have had to show younger students the difference between right and wrong.

<u>Sample Response</u>

'Yes, during my placement at PGCE, I had a good experience of this. I was assisting with a Year 3 Maths class. At the start of each lesson, students were required to hang their blazers on hooks by the door. Then at the end of each lesson, they came to collect them as they left.

As the lesson finished, I witnessed two pupils putting their hands into the blazer of another student, who was still packing his bag away at the back of the room. Katie and Henry were taking things out of the other student's pocket and putting them in their own pockets. As the other student, Josh, made his way over; they quickly hung the blazer back up on the rack and acted like nothing had happened.

I took immediate action. Asking Josh to stay for a moment, I approached Katie and Henry and asked them to explain their performance. Feigning ignorance, Katie pretended that she didn't know what I was talking about. Henry started to cry. He immediately admitted stealing from Josh's pockets and put the contents on the table. Katie did the same, but only after kicking Henry in the shins. I made the pair apologise to Josh, who left with his possessions.

I then sat down with Henry and Katie to discuss their behaviour. I explained to them that stealing in any form is wrong. I asked them to explain their behaviour. Henry said that he thought it would be funny, but was extremely repentant. He continued to cry. I acknowledged that he was genuinely sorry. I stated that there would be further consequences if he did it again. Katie also apologised, but called Henry a 'snitch' and continued to blame him for getting caught. I explained to Katie that stealing warrants a serious enough offence to call her parents. This seemed to have an immediate impact, as she started to cry too and pleaded with us not to. She apologised several times and promised that it would never happen again.

I finished the meeting by asking Henry and Katie to explain exactly why stealing is wrong. After they gave me a satisfactory explanation, I let them leave, but resolved to keep a close eye on the situation in future.'

Q50. Do you have any questions for me?

Once you hear this question, you'll have reached the end of the interview. However, this doesn't mean you can relax. There is one final hurdle to overcome, and that is YOUR questions.

When answering this question, the first thing to recognise is that you should never respond with 'no'. Why? Well, think about it like this. It's basic human nature to ask questions if you are interested. Therefore, a failure to ask questions at the end of an interview will indicate the exact opposite. Namely, that you aren't interested in finding out more about the school or the role.

Prior to your interview, write out a list of 6 or 7 questions to ask the interviewer. This way, even if one or two or even three of your questions are answered over the course of the interview, you'll still have questions to fall back on.

Sample questions YOU can ask

Q. What kind of age ranges will I be teaching to start off with?

Q. What are the opportunities like for progression in this role?

Q. Will there be an opportunity to get involved with extra-curricular activities?

Q. Do you have any doubts over my ability to perform the role?

Q. Will there be an induction period required before I start teaching?

Q. How big is the library at this school?

Chapter 4
The Classroom Survival Guide

Along with answering interview questions, many interviewers will also ask you to teach a practice lesson. This is so that they can assess how well you are actually able to teach, rather than how well you can talk about teaching! In many cases, the practice lesson will come before the interview itself. The reason for this is so that the interviewers can ask you questions based around your lesson. For example, you might be asked to assess how you felt the lesson went, and identify areas in which you struggled or were strongest in.

While we can't actually show you how to run a lesson in this book, we can give you some top pieces of advice for planning and executing your lesson to perfection.

Lesson Planning

Whether you are teaching for your interview or teaching a full lesson in a school, you need to be prepared. Lesson planning is one of the core competencies of teaching, and therefore it's essential that you can demonstrate this. Teaching is an extremely unpredictable job. You never know what problems are going to come up in the classroom, and you'll often be faced with issues that you quite simply would never have predicted.

So, how do you go about planning a lesson? Well, the first thing to consider is the subject material. You will generally be told in advance about what content you'll be expected to teach, so start brushing up as soon as possible..

Take a look at the lesson planning form below. This should give you a rough outline of the type of things that you'll need to consider when preparing for your own lesson. For the purposes of this, pick a particular topic and then work out how you would teach a lesson based around this topic, using the form as guidance.

LESSON PLANNING

SUBJECT	LEVEL	TUTOR	DATE	DURATION

OUTCOMES AND OBJECTIVES

1.

2.

3.

4.

RESOURCES REQUIRED:

_____

_____

_____

_____

_____

_____

ASSESSMENTS BEING USED:

Quizzes or exams _____

Self-assessments_____

Group exercises_____

Peer-assessments_____

Coursework_____

FEEDBACK ON ACTIVITIES:

WRITTEN   ORAL   GROUP   ONE-TO-ONE

BREAKDOWN OF LESSON:

INTRODUCTION:

LEARNING OBJECTIVES:

ACTIVITIES:

1.

2.

3.

EXTENSION ACTIVITIES:

DISCUSSION OF WHAT IS LEARNT:

ADDITIONAL SUPPORT DURING THE LESSON:

EVALUATE TEACHING PERFORMANCE

What went well?

How well did the students interact with the lesson?

What areas do you need to work on?

Is there anything that needs to be recovered in the next lesson?

Did your students understand everything being taught?

How can you adapt your teaching style if students didn't respond well to the lesson?

Was the lesson set to a high enough standard?

As a teacher, it's imperative that you have a substantial plan for every single lesson. This organisation will ensure that you will have as much control over the lesson as possible, maximising the amount of teaching time you have.

Getting knowledge across to students, whilst maintaining a good learning atmosphere, is very difficult. These aren't really things you can prepare for in advance, they are techniques and skills that are learned over time. If you haven't planned for the lesson then you will be juggling both of the above, with on-the-spot learning material. Fail to plan, and you are asking for trouble.

One of the most common reasons that lesson planning is so notoriously difficult is because of the time factor. Teachers are extremely busy, and it can be hard to find quality time to plan. Combined with marking and learning extra material; it can seem like quite a task to sit down and plan a detailed set of lessons. The reality is that the better and more detailed your lesson plans are, the easier everything else will be. If your lessons are running in a smooth and organised fashion, then you'll have less difficulties and less things to worry about. With this in mind, it's a good idea to schedule your lesson planning time around your own mind-set. If you know there is a particular time in the week where you are motivated and full of ideas, pick that as your lesson planning time.

Flexibility is also key. You need to make contingency plans for if things start to go wrong. At times, this might mean scrapping a certain part of your lesson plan (if you don't have enough time to run it) or even adding a bonus activity (if you finish things too fast). Be prepared for the unexpected, and remember that lessons are extremely unpredictable. As you gain more and more experience as a teacher, you'll find that it becomes easier to predict how long certain activities will run for; and will find it easier to incorporate small changes to your plan as and when needed.

Organising the room

The way your students are sitting in the room is really important. Very often, this can have a huge impact on the way in which the lesson pans out. Your seating plan should correspond with your teaching style. While you don't want to be rearranging the classroom for every lesson, the way you intend to teach needs to match the organisation of the room. For example, if you are a teacher who uses large amounts of group work, then you need to have students sitting fairly close to each other, so they can collaborate effectively. You also need to be able to move around the room and interact with different groups yourself. You could also use the circle seating approach, which is becoming more and more popular. By placing students in a circle, the focus becomes directly on interaction with the group, rather than simply interacting with the teacher.

Alternatively, if you are a teacher who doesn't use group work or peer-to-peer interaction, then you won't need to worry as much about this. However, you do need to ensure that you can see the whole class at all times, and that nobody feels isolated or is unable to see the front of the room. Problems like this are what typically lead to distraction and misbehaviour.

Using The Board

The board is one of the best tools available for teachers, and serves as the primary method of visual communication between the teacher and students. With this in mind, here are some guidelines to follow:

- Don't use the board too much, and don't spend the whole lesson writing on the board. This will mean that you spend too much time with your back to the class, which will lead to misbehaviour and distraction.

- Following on from the previous point, don't talk to the board! Communication between yourself and your students is vital, so you need to be talking directly to them. This is an easy mistake to make, but it's one you need to minimise.

- Use the board to engage the class. Make jokes about your poor handwriting, draw pictures, use it for games such as hangman.

- Remember that the board isn't the only option. To create a good learning atmosphere, you need to use a whole mix of tools, such as projectors or hand-held whiteboards (with dry wipe pens). After a while, just using one medium will become stale, so it's important to mix it up!

Interacting with the class

The way in which you interact with your class is extremely important. Fail to master this, and your lessons will quickly descend into chaos. There are some basic rules to follow that will keep your students as engaged as possible.

When speaking to the group, it's essential that you are talking loud enough for the whole class to hear. As we mentioned in the organisation section, if students can't hear or see you, they'll become distracted and start misbehaving. Speaking loudly and clearly is also important because it allows you to develop a clear sense of control and authority.

Obviously, yelling at the top of your voice won't do you any favours, but you need to make sure that it's clear that you can and will raise your voice if necessary. It's also important that you don't speak too quickly. This is a common problem, especially for newer teachers who are nervous.

Essentially, the key is to strike a balance. There are times when speaking slowly and clearly is appropriate (without patronising the students) but also times when it's necessary to speed things up. If you speak too slowly, the lesson will slow down and you might miss out on crucial content. Remember as well that you should assume students are listening to you. Don't speak to them as if they are already distracted or not interested, but at the same time don't speak without caring about whether they are listening or not.

Engaging Material

It's essential that you keep your lessons interesting, and make sure your students are focused and on track. Generally, the older students get, the more focused they become. This means that if you are teaching younger age groups; you can expect to deal with more distractions (although this isn't always the case!) This extends to talking and idle chatter too. Most teachers despair of this, but you can actually turn idle chatter to your advantage. Part of good teaching involves using real-life experiences as a platform for learning. Creating communication activities, where students can relate certain topics with ideas and situations from their own life; is a great way to minimise time wasted in the lesson.

Likewise, learning games are fantastic, provided they are organised properly. You can match these up with the communication activities, and introduce a fun competitive element. Students thrive on these kinds of exercises, as there is a figurative reward at the end of them. For example, you could ask two students to discuss a certain topic, before the class selects the winner. The list of exercises that you can use for this purpose is endless.

Part of your role as a teacher is in recognising when it's time to sit back a little, and relieve the pressure on the class. For example, showing them an educational film or video. Not all lessons have to be run under intense pressure; and there is a lot of value in giving your students activities that they genuinely enjoy. Often, these activities can be better for helping them to memorise information; as they'll associate this information with the task they found enjoyable – rather than blocking it out or forgetting it because it was boring. Remember also that a class which the students have enjoyed is far more likely to increase their interest in the subject in general; as it generates positive emotions. You should never make the mistake of judging how well your class went based on the popularity of the lesson; but ensuring that your students aren't bored will go a long way to determining how smoothly the lesson runs.

A Few Final Words...

You have now reached the end of your *Teacher Interview Questions and Answers* guide, and no doubt will feel more prepared to tackle the interview process. We hope you have found this guide an invaluable insight into the process, and understand what will be required of you.

For any type of selection process, we believe there are a few things to remember in order to better your chances and increase your overall performance.

REMEMBER – THE THREE P's!

1. **Preparation.** This may seem relatively obvious, but you will be surprised by how many people fail, because they lacked preparation and knowledge. You want to do your utmost to guarantee the best possible chance of succeeding. Be sure to conduct as much preparation as possible prior to your interview, to ensure that you are 100% prepared.

2. **Perseverance.** You are far more likely to succeed at something if you continuously set out to achieve it. Everybody comes across setbacks or obstacles in their life. The important thing to remember when this happens, is to use those setbacks and obstacles as a way of progressing. It is what you do with your past experiences that helps to determine your success in the future. If you fail at something, consider 'why' you have failed. This will allow you to improve and enhance your performance for next time.

3. **Performance.** Your performance will determine whether or not you are likely to succeed. Attributes that are often associated with performance are *self-belief, motivation* and *commitment.* Self-belief is important for anything you do in life. It allows you to recognise your own abilities and skills and believe that you can do well. Believing that you can do well is half the battle! Being fully motivated and committed is often difficult for some people, but we can assure you that nothing is gained without hard work and determination. If you want to succeed, you will need to put in that extra time and hard work!

Work hard, stay focused, and you achieve whatever you set your mind to!

Good luck with your teaching interview, and with all your future endeavours.

The how2become team

The How2become team

How2become have created this FANTASTIC guide to help you prepare for the tough teacher selection process.

Packed full of teacher training advice, application guidance, interview questions and even sample Professional Skills Tests, this guide is guaranteed to aid you during your preparation stages when applying to become a teacher.

Not only does this guide contain all of the above, but we also demonstrate the core competencies that you need to be focusing on in order to become a fantastic teacher.

FOR MORE INFORMATION ON OUR CAREER GUIDES, PLEASE CHECK OUT THE FOLLOWING:

WWW.HOW2BECOME.COM

WHY NOT PRACTICE FOR YOUR QTS!

FOR MORE INFORMATION ON OUR CAREER AND EDUCATIONAL RESOURCES, PLEASE CHECK OUT THE FOLLOWING:

WWW.HOW2BECOME.COM

Get Access To

FREE

Psychometric
Tests

**www.PsychometricTestsOnline.
co.uk**

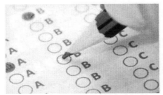